a new look at church growth

by
Floyd G. Bartel
with Richard Showalter

Faith and Life Press
Newton, Kansas

Mennonite Publishing House
Scottdale, Pennsylvania

Library of Congress Number 79-53523
International Standard Book Number 0-87303-027-3
Printed in the United States of America
Copyright © 1979 by Faith and Life Press, Newton, Kansas, and Mennonite Publishing House, Scottdale, Pennsylvania

Design by John Hiebert
Printing by Mennonite Press, Inc.

author's preface

Several consultations on church growth had been held in Mennonite circles in the mid-1970s. By 1977 it was felt that we needed a practical study of our own which could be used by local congregations better to understand the helpful learnings that were becoming available from church growth research and study. Soon after the General Conference Commission on Home Ministries assigned the task of writing this unit of study to me, Gordon Zook of the Mennonite Board of Congregational Ministries, Elkhart, inquired about the possibility of making it a joint project. Thus Richard Showalter was asked to join me in gathering material for the study, although I was still to do the writing. We also agreed to make it a joint publication for both the Mennonite Church and the General Conference.

I want to express appreciation to Richard Showalter, Gordon Zook, John R. Martin, Perry Yoder, Harold Bauman, Palmer Becker, Paul Isaak, Leonard Wiebe, and Elizabeth Yoder for reading and making helpful suggestions on the manuscript. A special thanks to Perry, Leonard, Palmer, and Paul who served as an editorial committee, and to Mary Regier for typing the manuscript. While I was writing, a group of my fellow members at Hesston Inter-Mennonite Church studied the chapters week by week. I want to thank them for the ideas those weekly sessions helped to spark.

This study is written with the confidence that God is teaching us all more in these days about how He gives growth. There are principles of growth we may not have understood in the past. May God guide us and enable us not only to recover our own Anabaptist vision more fully, but above all to serve Christ as Lord with greater faithfulness at home and abroad in our missionary task! My prayer is that working your way through this study will help you personally and corporately to have new eyes for growth and a renewed heart for outreach.

Floyd G. Bartel

foreword

A return to our Anabaptist roots is a return to joy in sharing our faith. The Anabaptist Church came into being by the conversion of people to Jesus Christ. It had no ethnic or cultural characteristics as such to which it invited people, but simply extended the fellowship of transformed lives.

In this sense the Anabaptists were truly the evangelicals of the Reformation. Their Biblicism had at its center a high Christology. The quality of their new life was a part of their proclamation, because they related ethics to Christology in the same way they related their salvation to Christology. They counted themselves expendable for the sake of the kingdom. Joy, love, and assurance, even in martyrdom, made their gospel attractive.

In his very significant work *A New Look at Church Growth,* Floyd G. Bartel is helping the twentieth-century Mennonite Church rediscover the Anabaptist vision in which discipleship relates directly to the evangelistic mission of Jesus Christ. He carefully relates evangelism to the character of the church, to holistic concerns, and to ethics. He has avoided a dichotomy between evangelism and social action by showing how the gospel while personal is also social. And a very important contribution is focusing for the church the place of planning and congregational involvement in sharing the gospel.

A significant question is raised as to whether or not our congregations are oriented to evangelism. Have we done serious planning to be a witnessing, growing congregation? Congregations should take seriously this emphasis on planning and staffing for evangelism as they have for nurture.

Discipling is not only a function for the in-group, but can also be a dynamic strategy of penetrating our immediate worlds with the good news of the kingdom. The local church is still God's primary means of reaching a given community.

Myron S. Augsburger, President
Eastern Mennonite College
April 1979   *Harrisonburg, VA 22801*

contents

introduction

The first thing to be said about church growth is that it is God who gives the growth. In 1 Corinthians 3:6 Paul says, "I planted, Apollos watered, but God gave the growth." We cannot cause growth. Growth is not something we produce. We can seek to understand it. We can work cooperatively with the Spirit of God to bring growth.

I am an avid gardener. I know that I cannot cause one thing in my garden to grow. But I also know that the things I do and how I do them make a lot of difference in the growth and fruitfulness of that garden. Similarly, there are principles of growth in the church which we can identify. One purpose of this study is to help us understand the principles of growth better. A second purpose is to help us develop the kind of attitudes and expectations for growth that Christ can use. He has promised in Matthew 16:18, "I will build my church." We want to be part of the fulfillment of that promise.

The fact of *church growth* is not new in the Christian movement. It has been part of the story of the church since its beginning as told in the book of Acts. Neither is church growth new in our own history. Mennonite churches come out of the Anabaptist movement in the Protestant Reformation of Europe in the sixteenth century. This rapidly growing movement sought to recapture the vision of the New Testament church and to restore the church of Acts in its day. It spread like a prairie fire across Europe.

After several decades, however, the Anabaptist movement settled down. In many places severe persecution had driven the movement into hiding. In the Low Countries where religious toleration came early, it flourished for awhile. But the movement never really spread beyond the context of Germanic cultures.

Thus, when later migrations of groups of Mennonites occurred, they took their German culture with them and became cultural, as well as religious enclaves within countries such as Prussia, Russia, America, Canada, and Paraguay, with little or no growth by evangelization of persons beyond their own families. The movement lost its original evangelistic thrust. For many generations almost the only source of growth, therefore, has been children of member families. Evangelism was replaced by nurture as the primary means of growth.

With our practice of believer's baptism and a theology that emphasized the necessity of repentance, conversion, and regeneration there has, however, remained the possibility that God might renew our evangelistic thrust. In more recent generations some of our congregations began to seek ways of reaching out. Sometimes new believers were evangelized. But often there were few results. There has been discouragement at times about our evangelism.

In recent years, however, God has been moving among us in new ways. All of the illustrations at the beginning of each chapter in this study come from Mennonite churches that are growing in remarkable ways! There are many more examples which time and space prevented including.

Church growth as a new movement today. While "church growth" is not new in the church or in our own history, the term is new in our vocabulary in a particular way in recent years because of the work of Donald McGavran. McGavran, a third generation missionary to India, began to ask, "Why do some churches grow and multiply while others do not?" As he gathered information and made observations, he began to see certain factors associated with growth and certain other factors often associated with nongrowth. In his books, *Bridges of God* (1955) and *Understanding Church Growth* (1970), he published those observations. His work deals with the overseas churches growing out of the work of European and North American missionaries. After growing interest in his work in North America, the Institute for American Church Growth was organized at Fuller Theological Seminary in 1972 to apply church growth research and observations to the churches of North America, and to teach its findings to North American church leaders. Since then "church growth" has become a movement in North America as well as a new term in our vocabulary.

Coming out of a fellowship which has long emphasized corporate and personal discipleship as essential, we are encouraged to hear McGavran and his colleagues insist that we must begin to count disciples rather than decisions in our evangelism. It is good to hear a renewed emphasis on the incorporation of new believers into the church. It is good to be reminded that the church must reclaim the task of evangelism.

Reclaiming evangelism as the task of the local church. Norman Kraus, Goshen College Center for Discipleship, once pointed out that churches have depended, in the past several decades, on the para-church organizations like the Billy Graham Crusade, Campus Crusade, etc., to do our evangelism for us. But the evangelistic task belongs to the local church. The incorporation rate of new converts into local churches out of the Billy Graham Seattle campaign in 1976, for example, was close to 7 percent. The incorporation rate of new believers in congregational evangelism typically runs from 50 to 60 percent.[1] This means that evangelism has a very high casualty rate. This should concern us because those who become the casualties can become harder to reach the next time with the gospel. Furthermore, to carry on evangelism apart from the context of the congregation contributes to a false understanding of the Christian faith as an individualistic affair just between "Jesus and me." Jesus said, "By this all men will know that you are my disciples, if you have love for one another" (John 13:35). The goal of evangelism is not only decisions, but also disciples who are being incorporated into the body of Christ, and nurtured, trained, and enabled to participate in the ongoing mission of God in the world.

Evangelism belongs in the context of the local church because it should not be isolated from the rest of Christian experience. It is hoped that this study might help to rekindle the vision for outreach in each local congregation that studies it. As Emil Brunner once said, the church exists by mission as fire exists by burning. All of our programs in the church can be revitalized by a new vision for outreach even as our evangelistic outreach itself may gain greater integrity because it is being carried on by local congregations.

To reclaim evangelism in our churches may mean acknowledging the biblical concern for salvation as well as discipleship in our emphasis. Jose M. Ortiz, writing in *Mission Focus,* January 1977, points out that Spanish language Mennonite churches are growing today because in the Menolatino churches salvation is the agenda. The altar is the place where the action is. Latino pastors tend to make their pulpits burning bushes where the fragrance of the Lord is felt. The altar is the place of conversion, vocational commitment, consecration, and prayer for healing and forgiveness. There is a lot of foot traffic at the altar. The net result is the reconciling, retaining, and recycling of people. Salvation is the agenda around which people circle even when the altar is taken to the street corners, the condominium, the parking lots, the factory, or the hospital halls.

A church that reclaims evangelism will have many entry points for new believers. Ralph Lebold, conference minister for the Ontario Mennonite churches, asks, "Where in our churches can people make a public declaration of their decision to follow Jesus? Many of our churches have moved away from the revival meeting and do not have an altar call in their worship services. Where are the points of entry and the vehicles for recognizing and calling for commitment? The annual membership classes are increasingly being rejected as a way to make commitments. Also, this vehicle has been geared more to helping our own children find faith than to helping the outsider. We must develop explicit vehicles if we want to help people make explicit commitments."[2]

There are signs that our local churches are reclaiming the task of evangelism. It is the purpose of this study to encourage that trend.

The local church and its world missionary vision. While the focus of this study is on the mission and growth of the local church, our vision of God's missionary purpose for us must always include the whole world. Some of our churches have responded generously in their giving of persons and resources

4

for the missionary task overseas. This is to be commended and encouraged. It is hoped that this study will also strengthen the world missionary vision for several reasons. First of all, as the local congregation becomes more mission oriented locally its mission beyond itself is strengthened. Secondly, the more mission oriented the local congregation becomes, the more effectively it functions as a setting in which we learn to be "missionaries"; and those who do follow the call to go to other cultures and other nations will be better prepared. Thirdly, we are rapidly entering an era in which Christian missionaries are not only sent by us, but also received from overseas churches. The missionary task will become more and more a task in which we will be called into new kinds of cooperative endeavors, new opportunities in which we who have remained in the "home church" can learn from our overseas brothers and sisters. An example of this currently is the beginning of several new Chinese Mennonite congregations next door to more traditional Mennonite churches in North America.

What do we mean by church growth? One question that will arise quickly in the minds of our readers is, "What is meant by church growth—numerical growth or spiritual growth?" It is our conviction, as we prepare this material, that both are important. Both are signs of a faithful church. *Acts* has more than twenty references to numerical growth. Most of them occur in close conjunction with some observation about the spiritual growth of the church as well. Numbers are used, not in a calculating way, but in a celebrative way. In this study we do look at numerical growth unapologetically, though also not as an end in itself. Church growth, in fact, should not necessarily become the center of our attention in the church. The center of our attention must continue to be Jesus Christ Himself. He is Lord of the church. He promised, "When I be lifted up, I will draw all men to myself." Our ultimate concern must always be faithfulness to Christ.

Numerical growth, however, can be one important indicator of our faithfulness in carrying out the Great Commission in obedience to Christ. Numerical growth is a concern of this study because we believe it is the will of God that all persons be brought into His kingdom under the lordship of Christ.

The church growth movement has emphasized the value of research and analysis for a better understanding of the dynamics that are at work in church growth. We have found that local churches who are willing to analyze and understand their own situation are often further enabled by the Spirit for their mission. We want to learn all we can in this way. However, we also want to acknowledge that no amount of sociological research will cause the church to grow. The church grows as persons committed to Jesus Christ and to one another are empowered by the Holy Spirit to carry out the mission Christ entrusted to us. Use this study and the exercises provided in the Leader's Guide to help you gain insights about your own situation, but do not assume that they are a substitute for the dynamic of the Holy Spirit at work in and through your congregation.

Four kinds of growth. Those who have been doing research in church growth speak of four kinds of growth: (1) internal growth, which refers to the spiritual maturing that occurs in the body of Christ—this includes the development of Christian family life so that children of Christian parents grow up in the faith to become part of the body of Christ in each new generation; (2) expansion growth, which refers to the kind of growth that comes from evangelism carried on by the local church—this means that new believers are being won and incorporated into the body of Christ out of non-Christian background; (3) extension growth, which refers to the planting of new congregations; (4) bridging growth, which occurs as the gospel is shared across cultural boundaries with persons of another racial, ethnic, or national identity. An example of this kind of growth would be our overseas mission program which we have carried on for more than a hundred years. Throughout this study various elements of all four of these types of growth will be examined.

How to use this study. There are two levels at which this study can be used. The first is to use it as a classroom study in which the class meets from week to week and discusses the content of each chapter. At this level it should take a minimum of thirteen weeks. Using it this way would help the group begin better to understand the principles of growth which can be identified in many growing churches. Church growth is complex. Not all growing churches show all the principles of growth, but some are evident in each vital growing church. Often a combination of principles can be observed in each situation. A basic goal of this study is an improved understanding of how growth takes place.

The second way to use this study is to take time also to use the involvement exercises suggested in the Leader's Guide which are designed to help a group make observations about its own situation. Using the material in this way would require twenty-six weeks. To gain some understanding of our own church and our own situation can help us to see more clearly what kinds of decisions and plans and action may be needed. We hope this study will help you decide whether or not you need to do a more thorough assessment, goal setting, and planning process as a next step.

This study is not a "how to do it" evangelism manual. It is more like a prerequisite for more specific training in outreach. Thus, following this study, the group may wish to take a further step involving the congregation in an assessment and goal-setting process; and then plan for more specific evangelism training, for example, in keeping with its outreach goals, along with the other goals you may have.

Additional resources for further study, or for goal setting or for training, are becoming available in the area of congregational mission, evangelism, and church growth. Some of these are listed at the back of this volume.

This study has been organized into three units. The first deals with the internal life of a congregation that grows. It is called "The Kind of Church that Grows." This unit looks at the marks of a church that is vital and alive spiritually. The second unit deals with the outreach dimension of growth. It is called "The Growing Church Reaches Out." The third unit is called "Encouraging Growth." It deals with some ways that a local congregation can analyze its own situation, make some new plans, and mobilize for growth. While each unit has four chapters, many of the chapters can be used individually for one topic. Or a series of four sessions using only one of the four units can be arranged in your schedule if that fits your need best.

Notes
[1]Win Arn, "Mass Evangelism, the Bottom Line," *Church Growth: America* (January-February, 1978), pp. 4-6, 16-18.
[2]"Evangelism in Dispersion," *The Mennonite* (October 25, 1977).

the kind of church that grows

chapter 1

examining
our motives

Church Growth Principle: *A growing congregation has a deliberate commitment to people beyond itself.*

How has Mountainview Mennonite Church, a congregation of 178 members, followed through on its clear commitment to people beyond themselves?

"At our annual meeting in January 1977 our congregation was led by God to devote more of our physical and spiritual energies to outreach into the immediate community," writes Sig Toews, chairman of the congregation. "In March of that year Les and Anne Klassen, members of Mountainview, accepted the call to coordinate our English outreach."

The congregation clearly designated Les as "Outreach Minister" and appointed a reference and support committee of three to work closely with him. Later in January 1979, it also sent him to a church growth institute in California for further training.

In June 1977 Stephen and Sally Lee joined the pastoral team of Paul Boschmann and Les Klassen to accept the assignment to plant the first Chinese Mennonite Church in North America in our community. The Mountainview congregation carried out a mailing to over 5,000 persons with Chinese names in its area of Vancouver. It offered its building to the new Chinese congregation which soon began to gather under Stephen's leadership.

By September of 1978 the new Chinese congregation itself had purchased the YWCA building in the heart of Chinatown and had not only begun meeting there but had also opened a counseling room, a combination Chinese library-bookstore-reading room, and a ministry to 5,000 new Chinese refugees. In addition, Stephen Lee has trained Thomas Yu as an apprentice, and the congregation has already commissioned him to plant a new Chinese Mennonite Church in Toronto. This Chinese Mennonite church planting ministry is also given support by the Canadian Mennonite Conference.

Nearly everyone wants to see the church grow. Very few would say, "No, I'd rather not see our church grow." Those who say "No" have various reasons, such as, "Our church is large enough as it is," or "We don't have room for more and we'd have to build," or "I don't think numbers are important in the church."

It is true that numbers for the sake of numbers are not important. But if we remember that each number represents a person, the numbers do become important. We have learned to keep careful financial records, not because financial statistics are important in themselves, but for other reasons. Someone has said that we need to become at least as concerned to keep "people statistics" as we are to keep "financial statistics."

Jesus instructed us to "make disciples of all nations." His parable of the sower in which some seed fell on good ground and produced one hundredfold suggests that it is the will of God that there should be many who respond and that they do so wholeheartedly. It was only as the Good Shepherd carefully counted His sheep that He realized that one out of a hundred was lost! God does not desire that there should be even one person who perishes. Our desire for the growth of the church is rooted in God's will that the lost all be found.

Growth in numbers is not only one of the evidences of faithful obedience to the Great Commission, but also an essential ingredient to qualitative or spiritual growth in our churches. The longer a congregation goes on without welcoming a new person into its midst, the more ingrown and closed it tends to become in its spiritual life. New Christians in our fellowship are God's gift to us, enriching our fellowship and widening our horizons!

Our ambivalence about growth. There are also those of us who say, "Yes, we'd like to see our church grow, but . . ." or, "We are in favor of growth if it is the right kind of growth." Usually we mean the right kind of people—people who will be an "asset" to our church, or people who think like we do, or people with the right kind of background so as not to exercise a wrong influence on our children.

There are still others of us who say, "Yes," but mean, "No." How do we do that? When we say we'd like to grow, but are convinced it cannot happen for us, or when we believe few if any people would really want to join our church, we are really saying, "No," to church growth. We may have assumed that we are a "peculiar" minority and cannot imagine others wanting to become what we are. We may see ourselves as a remnant church. We are not sure growth is important; we know that faithfulness is. But in reality both faithfulness and growth are important.

Another way some people say, "Yes," but mean, "No," is to insist that growth should be spontaneous, that it is not something to be planned for. It is assumed that because it is the work of the Holy Spirit it is more or less automatic. In fact, for some, planning for it feels like a lack of trust in the Lord. On the contrary, however, we plan for what we expect can really happen. The attitude of expectancy that God will keep His promise to build the church and bless the proclamation of His Word is one of the characteristics of growing churches. They plan accordingly! They look forward with hope and confidence. Good planning on our part can reflect hopeful and confident expectancy that God is alive and powerful—already at work to bring into being that which He has promised!

Sometimes we say, "Yes," with our mouths to the general question of growth, but say, "No," by refusing to participate. How we respond in specific and concrete ways reveals the real nature of our commitment. For example, we don't have time to get acquainted with new neighbors, or we don't "believe" in door-to-door visitation, or we never quite get around to inviting our friends to that group we enjoy. We may even say to ourselves, "When I get my own spiritual life strengthened, I'll begin to share my faith more. Once I get myself on a daily Bible reading and prayer schedule, I'll be more ready."

But some of us have been "strengthening ourselves" for many years! When will we know that we're "strong enough" to share with our neighbors and friends and family? We do need to nurture our own spiritual life, but as Christians we are not called to share out of our strength; we are called to share honestly, however weak or strong, that the glory may be Christ's and not our own. Paul knew this well in his experience. He said, "When I am weak, then I am strong" (2 Cor. 12:10).

The price of growth. The price of growth can be described in three ways. The first price of growth is *commitment.* When Jesus calls us to follow Him, He makes it clear that it will be costly (Mark 8:34). The costliness of commitment becomes evident as we become willing to put our general commitment to Christ into specifics that take time, energy, money, and ourselves.

For example, most of us have our lifelong circle of friends and relatives with whom we associate. Chances are, if we are Christians, they are also Christians. It takes time and thought for most of us to see and create the opportunities to get acquainted with new people who may not be Christians.

The second price of growth is *vulnerability.* Learning to share Christ with others in the opportunities we have will mean learning to let other people get to know us honestly—our warts as well as our good side. Most of us would rather make a good impression, even if it means keeping things superficial.

A third price of growth is *change.* New persons coming into a group will change it. They will not only make it larger, but they will also change it by adding their personalities to the personalities of those already in the group. To add people to a group changes the dynamics of the group and the whole group has to make adjustments. One of the common complaints of a few "old-timers" in a growing congregation is that they don't know everyone anymore.

We do not always see the changes that come with growth as a

blessing. When new people bring new needs, their presence makes new demands upon us. When new people bring new ideas, their thinking may clash with ours. When new people bring different backgrounds, we may feel they are strangers; they don't fit with our group. But Jesus makes it clear that our attitude toward the stranger will show our faith in Him. He says, "I was a stranger and you welcomed me" (Matt. 25:35).

The changes growth brings may also be unexpected. When our church begins to grow, others may be asked to do what we had been doing. They may do it differently than we did. Although we know we're supposed to be gracious about such things in church, we may be hurt. And I've seen "old-timers" leave the congregation when they were not re-elected to the office they had held. Yet the miracle of the Christian fellowship is that new persons *can* be added, and that the Holy Spirit enriches the fellowship with each new person added.

Motives for growth. Our real feelings about growth are often mixed. Let us examine the motives which may lie behind our interest in church growth.

Sometimes we develop a new interest in growth when we see our congregation decline. The desire for survival begins to stir within us. Lyle Schaller suggests that older people tend to be concerned that the church be around until they die. But survival is not an adequate motive for church growth.

Another common motive is the desire for success. I once read about two pastors who had a "friendly contest" going to see whose Sunday school attendance would be higher by the end of the year. It motivated them to extra effort because neither of them wanted to be a loser. There is a lot of pride at stake in being a "winner." The desire to succeed is strong in our society. It is deeply rooted in human nature. But success is not an adequate motive for church growth.

Some will say that the only worthy motive for growth is obedience to the Great Commission. Jesus said, "Go therefore and make disciples. . ." (Matt. 28:19). This is clearly a command of Christ. Obedience to Christ is to be taught and encouraged.

But how do we hear the command of Christ? Do we hear it as

a duty? Even a burdensome duty? Perhaps, as an obligation which also causes us to feel guilty when we fall short? How do we hear it? Do we already feel a tinge of guilt the moment we hear it? Maybe we have tried, at times, to be more faithful. But within ourselves we know how far we've fallen short of our intentions—and we feel even more guilty than before. We are almost caught in a cycle of guilt, renewed determination, failure, and more guilt. This is a counter-productive cycle, because guilt is one of the poorest motivations for positive action. Yet it is probably the one we most commonly stir up in one another in the church as we talk about growth or lack of growth.

How, then, do we hear the Great Commission? Would it be better to pretend it is not so important? Should we stop talking about it—or find some way to treat the Great Commission more lightly? Obviously not! Our Anabaptist forebears quoted these verses more often than any others!

I would like to suggest that we need to be set free in our own souls to hear and to obey the Great Commission. The vicious cycle of obligation, guilt, more obligation, and more guilt must be broken. Galatians 5:1 reminds us that Christ sets us free! He sets us free as we experience firsthand God's grace toward us in Christ.

The first and basic motivation for church growth comes from our own experience of salvation. Just how that happens varies from person to person. But only as the meaning of the gospel becomes personally real to us can we share it effectively.

David Schroeder, in his presentation at the Church Growth Consultation at Bluffton in 1976, observed that one of our difficulties is that we have made so many of the most important words of our faith vacuous—that is, without content. We have used words like "salvation," "born again," "redeemed," or "The Cross," but if we were asked precisely what is meant by them, we would be at a loss to give concreteness to the terms because they are not part of our experience.

When Jesus and the apostles used the terms "salvation" and "savior" they had something concrete in mind. The Exodus out of Egypt provided them with the language and imagery for communicating the gospel. This could be applied to new situations. As the people of Israel were redeemed from slavery in Egypt, so we are redeemed by the work of Christ from spiritual bondage to the "elemental spirits of the universe" (Gal. 4:3; Col. 2:15, 20; Rom. 3:24). Salvation is spoken of in concrete historical terms. An actual historical bondage (one that can be named and pointed to) has been broken and a new freedom, a new life, has come into being.

Salvation has to do with liberation; liberation from a bondage from which we cannot free ourselves. A bondage that we can name and identify but which in our own power we cannot escape. Yet when we give our testimonies of salvation we often name bondages to which we were never enslaved and from which we could not have been saved. Personal salvation is to have personally experienced the liberation in Christ from a specific bondage through surrender to Christ as Lord. When that happens, we can also speak of salvation in concrete terms of commitment. Commitment to Christ is the other side of surrender and liberation.

As Christians we tend further to restrict the term salvation in a way that Scripture does not. We tend to use it to describe only the initial turning to faith at conversion. And since many of us have not experienced a decisive turning point, we do not identify with an experience of salvation. It is in place there, certainly, but salvation is applied also to Christians. As Christians we are still in bondage to many things and need to be liberated to serve Christ. Our commitment to Christ needs to be made concrete and specific in more and more new ways as the Holy Spirit and Scripture continue to enlighten and deepen our understanding. Thus salvation applies to having been saved (Titus 3:5), to being saved (1 Cor. 1:18), and to the future when we will be saved (1 Peter 1:5).

My own experience illustrates what Schroeder explains. I had grown up a Mennonite. I knew the church as a warm and affirming fellowship. I learned well the way of discipleship and pursued it seriously. But I can also say with Paul (in Phil. 3:4-8, paraphrasing), "If anyone thought he had it made, I certainly did: baptized at age thirteen, of the people of Menno, of the tribe of Bartel (a good Mennonite name), a Mennonite born of Mennonites; well trained in the traditions of my church in all the right schools; so conscientious in my objection to war I almost refused to register for the draft; as to uprightness of life I neither smoked nor drank nor caroused as sinners do. But after I was out of seminary two years, the Lord, through an experience of profound failure, opened my eyes to see some of my own bondage to things like low self-esteem, deep-seated hostility, and self-righteousness; and showed me in a fresh way the wonder of His grace in Christ Jesus by which He sets us free. At various points in my life, when I have been made aware of my own bondage in some new ways and brought to the point of repentance and faith, God's promised gift of new freedom in the Holy Spirit has been fulfilled afresh. Salvation has become real for me in my life; it is being renewed and deepened from time to time; and I look forward with assurance and hope to the future."

As God's mercy and renewing power become increasingly meaningful to us, we will want to share them. Paul says, "The love of Christ overwhelms us" (2 Cor. 5:14, *Jerusalem Bible*). In 2 Corinthians 5:18, 19 he says that God first reconciled us to Himself and thus gave us the ministry and the message of reconciliation. As part of this firsthand relationship with Christ we also see other elements which are basic to our motivation. Paul often uses the phrase "we know." In 2 Corinthians 5:14 he says, ". . . for we are convinced. . . ." God gives us a deep inner confidence in Christ that gives us stability in the faith and the courage to persevere in the face of disappointments. Having trusted Him, we desire to serve Him. We hear in a new way the call of Christ to "follow me and I will make you fishers of men."

Once we get to know Christ personally, His love is shed abroad in our hearts through the Holy Spirit (Rom. 5:5) and the love of Christ controls—motivates—us (2 Cor. 5:14). The guilt-producing cycle of sense of duty, good intention, failure, and guilt is broken and we are set free to obey the Great Commission and to share the good news of Jesus, inviting others to join us in the way of the disciple as fellow disciples.

Our conscious desire may not be so much for growth as it is a desire to share with others the good news of Jesus Christ in caring ways of word and deed so that they may know Him and the abundant life He gives. Paul said, "Woe is me if I preach not the gospel!" He felt an eagerness within that made him alert to opportunities to share Christ that he would otherwise not have seen.

This eagerness within is illustrated by the story of Peter and John in Acts 3. They had probably seen the lame man at the temple gate many times as they passed by, for he was carried to this spot by his friends daily (Acts 3:2). But now they *saw* him with their hearts and stopped to minister to him.

Jesus had a deep desire to gather God's people into His arms, as it were, and bring them home to the Father (Luke 13:34). He looked out upon the crowd that followed Him and was moved with compassion toward the people, for they were as sheep without a shepherd. He saw the fields white unto harvest (Luke 10:2; John 4:35), but was concerned that the laborers were few!

What is a desire for the growth of the church? It is loving and caring about people as Jesus did! It is praying for more laborers to help with the harvest. It is an inner eagerness to reach out to others with love and the good news of reconciliation that will make them His friends also (2 Cor. 5:20, TEV). It is an inner attitude that is stirred by the Holy Spirit Himself dwelling within us. It is an inner desire that gives us new eyes to see. It is a new perspective that informs our decisions.

Motivation for mission is to be a shared motivation. Hebrews 10:24 reminds us to "stir up one another to love and good works." The call of God upon our lives in the Great Commission is not given to us simply as individuals. It is given to each congregation and to the whole church as a corporate commission and a common task.

God uses each of us to help motivate and encourage one another. Jesus calls us to a common commitment to make disciples, baptize them, and teach them to observe all things He has taught us in the knowledge and assurance that He Himself as Lord abides with us always. In the chapters which follow we shall examine a number of implications in such a deliberate corporate commitment to Jesus as Lord and to the mission He gives us in the world.

DISCUSSION

1. Read 2 Corinthians 5:11-20. Identify as many ways as you can in which Paul refers to Christian motivation in this passage.
2. Can you identify some of the various underlying motivations in the church for growth?
3. Is the church free to appeal to any kind of motivation so long as it gets results? Discuss the relationship between motivation and end results.
4. Jesus portrays God as the searching woman and the searching father of the lost son (Luke 15). What evidence does my life give of being in tune with this desire of the heavenly Father?
5. What do you think might be the price of growth for your church? For you personally?
6. Which of these statements have you heard? How do you react to each of them?

   _____ "Our church is large enough as it is."

   _____ "I'd favor building to make room for more people."

   _____ "I don't think numbers are important in the church."

   _____ "We'll need more new members soon, otherwise we'll have to close our doors."

   _____ "We like this church because it's small."

   _____ "I don't think a Mennonite church can grow."

   _____ "I don't know why we haven't been growing."

   _____ "I think we have more potential for growth than we've realized."

chapter 2

being clear
about our purpose

Church Growth Principle: *A growing congregation knows clearly why it exists.*

Hopewell Mennonite Church has experienced a 50 percent growth rate per year since 1975. Once a struggling semi-rural congregation of about fifty, stalemated with conflict, today it averages 340 in attendance.

What happened to change its direction? The members clarified their identity when they drew up their new membership covenant in which they defined what was expected of members: "A conversion experience, willingness to testify to it, accept the Bible as the Word of God, practice believer's baptism, attend on a regular basis, give systematically, give and receive counsel, take marriage seriously, and live a lifestyle based on love."

First among several factors Merle Stoltzfus, the pastor, now lists to account for their growth is a genuine concern and prayer for the unsaved. As pastor he himself spends a lot of time visiting, some of it in local restaurants and bars. One local bar owner and his wife, after they became Christians, closed the bar in their hotel which has become a meeting place for regular Bible study and prayer.

At Hopewell people emphasize an atmosphere of love and acceptance, nurture in small groups, a positive attitude, and training for evangelism. But first of all is their concern to reach the people around them. They know why they exist as a church.

20

① *A clear sense of purpose and mission.* It is clear from the New Testament that the church exists for an important purpose. A crucial question is: How well does the local congregation know what that purpose is? How strongly does the local church sense the importance of that purpose? In other words, does the congregation itself know why it exists? Many congregations have a statement of purpose near the beginning of their constitution. But if one asks the membership what it is, few, if any, can tell you.

Those who are leaders have a responsibility to clarify and reiterate the purpose of a congregation's existence. The apostles in the New Testament church took very seriously the statement of purpose Jesus had given them (as for example, in Matt. 28:19, 20 or Acts 1:8). Soon the good news of Jesus spread to many parts of the earth! To take seriously the purpose our Lord has given us for the church would firm up the basic conviction that growth is normative for the church, not exceptional.

② *A better balance between nurture and mission.* Our Anabaptist forebears argued with their state church contemporaries, who practiced infant baptism, that Jesus commanded us in the Great Commission, first to "make disciples," then to "baptize" them. Baptizing infants, they insisted, reversed the order of Christ's command.

In our experience four and a half centuries later, the issue is not simply that the order has been reversed, but that the nurture part of the Great Commission has largely overshadowed the outreach dimension. Nurture of those already in the congregation receives nearly all of our attention, time, and effort. Calling new disciples gets too little attention.

A little over one hundred years ago Mennonites began to hear the Great Commission once more. We heard it as a call to send missionaries to the heathen in faraway places. We have begun to hear it in recent years also as a local call. This is certainly true to the meaning of the commission as Jesus gave it. Literally translated from the Greek, the first verb, *go,* of the Great Commission in Matthew 28:19, 20 is not an imperative as many translations have made it. Only the verb *make* in *make*

21

disciples is an imperative. The verb used for *go* is a participle and is better translated *as you go,* or *as you are going.* Literally, it would be *going, therefore, . . .* but a participle at the beginning of a sentence is difficult to translate, hence, it has usually been translated *go.* This has, however, given us the impression that obedience to the Great Commission begins as we go somewhere away from home in order to make disciples. The true meaning is that we are commissioned to make disciples at home as well as wherever we go!

The priority of nurture and institutional maintenance over outreach is one that seems to come with age. At first, a new congregation is usually enthusiastically aware of the purpose for which it has been called into being as a church. But as time goes on, its organization develops, a building may be built, the members grow older, second- and third-generation Christians grow up within the church, and there is an almost unnoticed settling down—a drift toward greater concern for preservation and maintenance than for serving the missionary purpose for which the church was originally called into being. This tendency is sometimes referred to as "institutional drift." Someone has warned that the more intangible the results of the purpose for which we exist as a group, the more important it is to clarify and reiterate that purpose often and to shape clear goals regularly, lest we become increasingly self-serving as institutions, having the forms of religion, but without the power of the Holy Spirit.

One of the times a congregation moves away from mission goals to maintenance goals is when it moves into its own permanent building. The building itself is such a visible and commanding goal that when it is completed, the sense of completion leaves a congregation both satisfied and without a clear sense of continuing goals. Often without realizing it, the shift from mission goals to a maintenance orientation begins. The outreach tapers off and the growth of the congregation levels off.

Another point at which the shift toward maintenance can happen is in the hiring of a second staff person to serve as a minister of Christian education. Church growth researchers

22

uncovered this tendency in enough formerly growing churches that they investigated the reasons. They found that the pull toward maintenance and nurture is strong enough in most churches that when a staff person is hired for nurture, it tips the balance away from evangelism to nurture, and growth stops. It has been suggested that the second pastoral staff person should rather be a minister of outreach and the third staff person a minister of Christian education.

Nurture is needed. But the biblical balance would give evangelism greater attention than we often have. Can we rediscover and practice, as our Anabaptist forebears did, the evangelistic dimension of disciplemaking in the Great Commission?

It is often difficult for long-established congregations with a maintenance orientation to return to a more balanced nurture and mission oriented purpose. As such a change begins to happen, some members will change more quickly than others, and the difference in the way people see the reason for their church's existence results in tensions. This makes it difficult to work together in planning and carrying out programs. To unite behind a more missionary purpose requires leadership with vision and courage. It will require much prayer and open discussion. Even then it will not be easy to shift priorities from maintenance to mission as the Holy Spirit leads. Lyle Schaller, a well-known consultant to churches, observes that only one out of three are able to make the shift.

Clarifying our sense of purpose. Does your church have a congregational statement of purpose? Do more than half of your elected leaders know where to find it? Even more important, does the congregation have a fairly clear knowledge of what it is? You may decide to work on clarifying your purpose. A committee, especially selected for this task, may need to review your church's statement of purpose, report its findings, and guide the congregation through a process of sharpening your sense of purpose. Calling on an experienced church leader outside your congregation for counsel can be helpful.

If the purpose statement is well written, the following five questions will be answered affirmatively: (1) Is it biblical? (2) Does it state the basic reasons for your church's existence without necessarily listing specific structures or programs? (Programs and organizations may change, but our purpose is rooted in the Scriptures and the unchanging purpose of God for the church.) (3) Does it speak of your vertical relationship to God? (4) Does it say something about the internal life of the church? (5) Does it clearly state the outreach mission of the church?

In one congregation church board members decided they needed to rethink their purpose because their outreach was not working out well. They began by doing some research about their situation, but at the same time devoted themselves for three meetings to prayer and Bible study to clarify their purpose in outreach as a congregation. They concluded that they existed "to be a channel for God's love." This expressed the outreach dimension of their purpose very succinctly. It became the plumb line against which all their outreach programs were evaluated. Such a recovery of the outreach dimension of the Great Commission and a careful evaluation of how they were doing was for them the first step toward a doubling of membership through outreach in the next nine years.

A sense of identity. One important reason for sharpening our sense of purpose is that our own sense of who we are grows out of our sense of purpose. Dean Kelly, in his book *Why Conservative Churches Are Growing,*[1] suggests that it is those congregations with strict membership standards rather than those with lenient entrance requirements which are most likely to grow. He lists traits of strictness such as absolutism, conformity to church standards, and fanaticism as characteristics of churches which are growing; on the other hand, traits of leniency such as relativism, diversity, and dialogue are characteristics of churches which are not growing. He observes that ecumenically oriented churches or churches which belong to a denomination formed out of a denominational merger tend not to grow. In other words, those congregations which know what they believe and why they exist, he says, will be more likely to grow than those who permit diversity of belief. According to Kelly, a church which has a clear set of behavioral expectations of its members, even though they are limited in scope, is more likely to grow than the church which tries to be broad in its dealing with the many issues that we face in life. For example, a congregation might forbid its members to smoke, drink alcoholic beverages, use profanity, dance, or gamble. Their list of "dos" and "don'ts" may not be comprehensive, but they are simple and clear. They emphasize these few expectations over and over in various ways.

Kelly also suggests that conservative churches have grown because they have specialized their message on offering salvation, a message unique to the church. While many other modern-day organizations emphasize service, or benevolent fund raising, or socialization, or recreational opportunities, only the church has the message of salvation to offer. Those churches which specialize in the salvation message are not competing with a host of other organizations in what they offer and, therefore, are more likely to grow.

While Kelly's observations are persuasive, another way of understanding what he sees in conservative churches is in terms of a clear "sense of identity." The conservative churches he describes seem to have a clearer sense of who they are in what they believe and what they stand for. Thus, people outside those churches can also feel that they know what this church believes, what is expected, and what steps are required for entry. These churches grow partly because people are more likely to commit themselves to a group whose identity is clearly projected to those around it than they will to a group that does not seem to be clear about what it stands for! People seem to like to know what they're getting into. There is a more secure feeling about joining such a church, even when its message is narrowly limited and its theology may not be sound, than in joining one where much seems nebulous and open to questions. What ecumenically minded congregations or merged congregations often face is an identity crisis. They are often not clear themselves about what they really believe or stand for. Are we clear about our message? Are we clear about our purpose?

Who will know how to respond unless the bugle gives a clear signal (1 Cor. 14:8)?

Our identity is derived from our purpose and the way we ourselves understand the Christian message. It is not the result of a public relations campaign. Clarifying our message and our purpose in a statement is one way to begin to clarify who we are. Knowing our own history and the experiences that have shaped us can be helpful, but the Scriptures are our primary source.

Our statement of purpose is not to be put on a shelf. It is only a beginning step in taking the claims of Christ upon ourselves as members and as congregations more seriously—as seriously as the way of the cross calls us to be about our purpose in this world. This does not mean a return to legalism. It does not mean limiting our message. It means focusing and communicating clearly. It does not mean overly narrowing our commitment for the sake of clarity. But it may mean being willing, in a new way, to face what it means to be a missionary church in these days.

You may wish to reflect on our own sense of identity. What is it? Where does it come from? The following are several characteristics which seem strong in describing our call and character as Mennonite churches:

1. We are a people with a strong sense of being God's people under the lordship of Christ. A favorite passage of our forebears was 1 Peter 2:10: "Once you were no people but now you are God's people." We stress the necessity of conversion and regeneration as new persons are brought into the Christian life and the fellowship of the church. Voluntary commitment is important. Believer's baptism symbolized our understanding of coming into the church, as well as coming to faith in Christ.

2. We are a biblical people. The Bible, interpreted in the light of Christ, is our authority for faith and practice.

3. We are Christ-following people—called to a life of discipleship which takes the life and teachings of Jesus in passages like the Sermon on the Mount seriously, as well as His birth, death, and resurrection. This means we are a people for whom the way of discipleship means that we live the life of a

peacemaker in the world. We are a people of compassion, emphasizing mutual aid to one another and service to others in our world. Our sense of mission is guided by Jesus' call to "love as I have loved you."

DISCUSSION

1. As a Bible study, review the Great Commission statements as found in Matthew 28:19, 20; Mark 16:15; Luke 24:45-49; John 20:21-23; Acts 1:8; and 2 Corinthians 5:18-20. Note the main emphasis of each. What do these various versions of the Great Commission tell us about the purpose of the church?

2. Below is a series of comments made by people about their church. Can you identify which of them reflect a *maintenance purpose* and which a *mission purpose,* and tell why you think so?

    a. "I'd be glad to see the weekday child-care program continue to use the children's unit of our church building. Does it still meet their needs?"

    b. "Have you seen what's happening to the walls in that one room the child-care program uses? We'll have to paint every year at this rate!"

    c. "I would like to see these new folks who are moving into these old homes around our church on Sunday morning. Our door is wide open; we have plenty of room, and they know they are welcome. All they have to do is walk in."

    d. After church: "Good morning, pastor. It's been over six months since you were out to see me. Pastor Schmidt used to stop in once a month when he was here."

    e. "Look at those kids chasing each other up and down the front church steps. They shouldn't be doing that. There's one sliding down the porch railing. Isn't there any place else they can chase one another?"

    f. "We need to find a way to welcome new people moving into our area as soon as they arrive, with a helping hand, help with some local information, or a gift of food for a meal to let them know we care and want them to feel at home here."

    g. "I was sort of hoping the Jones family would come to our church. They're both very talented. They'd be a real asset to our church."

    h. "It's really great to see Tom and Dorothy's class of young couples crowding out their room. We'll either have to help

27

them find a bigger room to meet or help start another class."

i. "How can Pastor Bob get out and visit everyone in this neighborhood if we expect him to attend every meeting there is here at church?"

j. "Jim, since you know Mr. Johnson (Steve's employer), can you talk to him tomorrow about what happened to cause Steve to lose his job? Steve is not a member here, but if the family is seriously in need, let's see how we can help."

k. "Last year we spent $5,000 on the youth program. Mike, our summer student intern, got a lot of kids together. I happen to know some of our own youth did not participate. I think we should first get a program going that would involve all our own youth."

l. "I'm not in favor of relocating to a larger new building. Let's see how we can enlarge this one."

3. Ask the members of your class to write down how they remember your congregational statement of purpose (if you have one) or how they would state it themselves.

Notes

[1] Dean M. Kelly, *Why Conservative Churches Are Growing* (New York: Harper and Row, 1962), pp. 78-96.

chapter 3

an internal climate for growth

Church Growth Principle: *A growing congregation has a climate within that accepts and affirms new persons.*

From 1972 to 1979, the English Lake Church (English Lake, Indiana) has grown from 35 to 200 in Sunday morning attendance. Across the community English Lake has gained a reputation as a loving, caring fellowship and an exciting place to worship.

When asked why the church is growing, Elder Sam Fugate was quick to respond, "The basic reason is openness to the Holy Spirit."

Pastor Art Good, member of the Missions Commission of the Indiana-Michigan Mennonite Conference, agrees. "A lot of factors contribute to church growth. But we really began to grow as the Spirit was free to meet all kinds of needs in all kinds of ways—salvation, healing, cleansing, encouragement, understanding, power for service.

"Our goal is that each person becomes *complete in Christ.*"

A frequent testimony. Have you heard new members from growing churches share why they became members? You might have heard responses like these:

"We decided to visit one Sunday soon after we moved into the area. The people were so friendly we felt at home from the start."

"We had been shopping around for a church, but when we attended Bethel it was different. There was something about the atmosphere there that made you want to come back."

"We visited two Sundays and had three invitations to be part of a home fellowship group! We went, and today we are members. In the smaller home fellowship group we soon had a new circle of friends, even though we still don't know everyone in the congregation."

Such are some of the testimonies of new members in churches that have an accepting and affirming climate.

At a conference on church growth where new members shared how and why they had become members of growing churches, one after another said in some way, "I'm a member in my church because I felt truly loved and accepted."

How a negative climate hinders. Sometimes, however, a negative climate prevails. A negative climate is characterized by such things as rigidity, defensiveness, exclusivism, faultfinding, or a moralistic approach to Christian living. It is curious that we should attach so much importance in some churches, for example, to things having to do with appearance, while we almost completely overlook negative and faultfinding attitudes which are destructive of other persons.

Sometimes the preaching fosters a negative climate. When the preaching majors in criticism, or when the preaching is moralistic, preoccupied with "dos" and "don'ts" of the Christian life (especially the "don'ts")—it builds a negative climate. A gallup poll conducted for twenty-nine religious groups in April 1978 quotes 41 percent of those polled who are nonchurchgoers as saying they would attend if they could find a trusting clergyman who preached well.

A negative climate is expressed in a high level of resistance among the members to any changes. The level of suspicion and mistrust is also high. It is risky to suggest a new way of doing things. Socializing among members tends to be minimal. There is an undercurrent of fear—fear that one might be caught saying or doing the wrong thing. The Christian life is understood very individualistically.

Needless to say, such conditions will not be very inviting to the new person whose heart hungers for good news, friendship, and hope. New persons may experience such a congregation as cold and unfriendly without being able necessarily to explain why they feel that way. The internal climate is extremely important for growth because it is often our first witness to the stranger in our midst.

How the New Testament speaks of the internal climate for growth. The New Testament speaks of the internal climate of the church as fellowship. We have used the term for various kinds of socializing. But the New Testament term for fellowship comes from the Greek word *koinonia.* Although socializing is included in the meaning, *koinonia* means more as it is used in the New Testament. It means living the new commandment of Jesus when He said, "Love one another." As described in passages like Galatians 6:1-10, Ephesians 5:1-21, Philippians 2:1-13, Colossians 3:1-17, it is not something we achieve by group effort. It is rather the result of and the evidence of the Holy Spirit's transforming work in our lives and relationships to bring us together in a new way.

Our coming together as a people can be superficial and casual or it can be personally and spiritually meaningful. Such a new quality of togetherness is an essential part of our witness to the world. This was true of the early church as described in Acts 2:41-47 and 4:32-37. In the midst of that Jerusalem population with its many parties and factions and its atmosphere of suspicion and mistrust, the day of Pentecost brought a powerfully revolutionary expression of community. People were changed. Relationships were transformed. The Lord brought them together in a new way. It made a profound impression "and the Lord added to their number day by day those who were being saved" (2:47).

Thus it was again in the sixteenth century with our own forebears in the Anabaptist movement. Noblemen and peasants were drawn together in *koinonia.* It was this coming together across lines of class and status, however, that caused state and church authorities to bring severe persecution upon the Anabaptists. This new movement was accused of destroying the order of society. The late H. S. Bender, a leading

31

American Mennonite historian, has said that the first test of the church is not merely to proclaim the availability of redemption (as the Protestant reformers did) but to demonstrate in its life what redemption is.[1]

Studies have shown that the most pervasive needs experienced by people in North America today grow out of their sense of loneliness. As a church we have the opportunity to reflect a divine fellowship to a lonely world that is weary of superficial "togetherness."

Acceptance of "outsiders" is crucial. Sometimes the internal climate is warm and accepting of "insiders" but strangers still feel very much excluded. Churches who have many members with relatives in the same congregation often engage in socializing that leaves the outsider feeling very much on the outside. It's almost as if the only way you can get into such a congregation is by being born into it or marrying into it.

The same strong "insider-outsider" feelings are heightened when the culture and customs of those inside the church are quite distinct. The internal climate may be warm and accepting, but some outsiders wonder how to get in. They say, in one way or another, "I admire the relationships and closeness that you have. You really take care of each other! The question I have is, 'How do you get in?'"[2]

Sometimes a congregation thinks of itself as an accepting and affirming fellowship, but the real message given to new persons is different. One congregation had a visitation program to reach persons in its community. Some of the new persons who had been won to the Lord began to attend at the Sunday worship hour. But after several years almost none of them had joined. After attending for a little while they usually stopped coming. When church board members were interviewing a young pastoral candidate, they told him they were puzzled and discouraged about their outreach, and wondered whether he had any ideas about what could be done.

He suggested that the people who had come and then stopped coming might be best able to tell them what the problem was. So the church board asked the new pastor to locate and interview as many of these people as he could. As he did, one theme kept recurring. They said, "There didn't seem to be a place for us there," or "We were not needed there," or, as one man put it rather bluntly, "I'd have to say we were frozen out!"

The church board was surprised when the pastor reported this because the people thought of themselves as a friendly church. They tried to be sure to greet visitors warmly on Sundays. They even had "greeters" at the door so no one would be missed! But as they thought and prayed further about what these folks had told them, they began to recognize that there is a difference between being friendly and being friends.

How a caring climate helps us grow. One of the important evidences of God's transforming grace in our lives is to be seen in the way we treat people who are different from ourselves— the poor, the outcast, the prisoner, the mentally ill, the stranger. Jesus, in Matthew 25, makes this a key test of how we relate to Him!

Churches with a visitation evangelism program or regular altar calls do not necessarily grow. While new people may respond, they may also be leaving by the "back door" as fast as they come in through the "front door" if there is no attention given to fellowship, personal growth needs, and training for witness and service. Thus, some important questions for any church to ask itself at any time are, "Where are our new members of the last five years? Are most of them participating or have they 'disappeared'?" Without assimilation of new members, congregational evangelism also leaves many casualties.

A study of churches in the Upper New York Synod of the Lutheran Church in America showed that the difference between growing and declining congregations was essentially a matter of how well the congregation retained its members. Retention seemed to depend largely on the quality of the internal relational life in the congregations. This proved to be a more significant factor than their evangelism efforts![3]

The percentage of inactive members tends to grow as a congregation gets older. But the percentage of the membership living in the immediate community which is inactive is also one of the indicators of the quality of caring that prevails in a given congregation. This, too, is one of the marks of faithfulness as well as a contributing factor in the growth of the church. Reaching the inactive members is often a difficult and neglected ministry!

Revitalizing the internal climate for growth. How can a church which may have become very traditional, or highly formal, or legalistic, or routine and uneventful be revitalized? Sometimes we feel like asking with Ezekiel, "Can these bones live again?"

We have the promise of the Holy Spirit (Acts 2:39) for each generation. The Holy Spirit needs to be given a chance. But how? Perhaps some illustrations will serve best to answer that question because there is usually something unique in each situation.

1. In one congregation the new pastor began by inviting one lay leader in to listen as he shared out of his own life and pilgrimage. After the visit, the lay leader asked for a chance to do the same. They met again. They became partners in prayer. One by one others became part of that sharing and prayer circle. And as the leadership of that congregation was renewed, the church began to come alive also.

2. Another pastor used a leader's retreat setting, soon after his arrival, to begin to share. The entire retreat was spent in sharing out of these people's lives in order to learn to know and care about one another. The emphasis was on getting their own lives opened to the ministry of the Holy Spirit and to one another. Some churches find an annual leaders' retreat for reflection and renewal very helpful.

3. Still another new pastor invited the congregation in groups of twelve to fifteen to his house where he and his wife had a chance to get acquainted with them and introduce themselves. They shared their personal pilgrimage of faith. In a low key way he also gave them a chance to reflect on where they were in their pilgrimage. Out of those get-acquainted meetings, over half the membership came to a new assurance of salvation in their own lives. The church began to come alive!

4. In one church some congregations have adopted the goal

of having every married couple in the congregation attend a Marriage Encounter weekend because they find that as marriages are renewed God also begins to renew the whole church to relate in more loving ways.

5. In a small congregation of mostly older people a turning point came when it was the only congregation in the community to welcome the "hippies," as the counter-culture youth of the sixties and early seventies were often called. They not only welcomed them, but showed them love and sought meaningful ways to share the gospel with them. Two of them were converted to Christ. This became the beginning of a new era for that church.

6. The Lay Witness Weekend has been a turning point for a number of congregations. As visiting witnesses share out of their Christian experience, the Lord has had opportunity to touch the lives of longtime believers in new ways as well as to reach the hearts of some who have never made a personal commitment to Christ. New first-time commitments to Christ, new freedom to share, and deeper renewal of standing commitments are often the result.

7. In another congregation, one turning point of renewal came in a fall preaching series by a guest minister. There had been such preaching series a number of times before, but this time the Holy Spirit found opportunity to minister to hearts in new ways. Several persons in the congregation experienced reconciliation. New families were brought into the fellowship. The congregation had had a time for sharing in the morning service for several years before, but now people began to use it!

The way of renewal is also risky. To open our hearts to the Holy Spirit will bring changes. We often fear changes and resist them. A renewal event may also bring renewal to some and not to others.

Renewal comes to different persons in different ways. For some it may happen through a new encounter with a caring small group. For others it may happen as the Word is proclaimed and taught with freshness and reality. For some renewal has come through a school experience with a gifted teacher. For some renewal has come through a Marriage

Encounter weekend. For still others renewal has come in the midst of a special service assignment. But while spiritual renewal may come into our lives in a variety of ways, our tendency is to expect everyone else to experience renewal the same way we did. Can we, instead, affirm the work of the Holy Spirit in the life of a brother or sister even though it may not have happened to them in the same way as to us?

Renewal brings new joy and enthusiasm. But the deeper evidence of renewal is to be seen in the extent to which the *fruits* of the Spirit (Gal. 5:22, 23) become evident! Is there a greater maturity in love, peace, patience, kindness, goodness, faithfulness, gentleness, self-control, as well as new enthusiasm and commitment?

While each person in the congregation needs to understand the risks as well as the joys of renewal, the pastor often has a key role. If the pastor strongly opposes a particular experience, such as charismatic renewal, he or she can make it more difficult for those in whose lives the Holy Spirit is at work through that way of renewal. Some may leave the congregation. Growth is hindered. If, on the other hand, the pastor identifies totally with those experiencing renewal and becomes such an advocate of a particular renewal movement as to suggest that persons not touched in that way are not growing in their spiritual lives, he or she may help to cause a congregational split. Why? Because those who are not currently caught up in the renewal feel increasingly distant from the pastor when he or she identifies with a certain "group" in the congregation. Much of what happens at this deeper feeling level is not readily understood nor dealt with openly and helpfully. Thus, even ordinary conflict situations now take on different meanings, and greater polarization develops. A power struggle may build until a split occurs.

What is the alternative? Should the pastor avoid opening up his or her life to the Spirit's renewing work? Definitely not! I have repeatedly heard pastors of growing churches testify that it was only after the Holy Spirit brought them through their own transforming "wilderness pilgrimage" with its pain, its healing, and its joy, that they were set free to be more sensitive and more truly available in God's calling for them. I can testify to that myself. The pastor's own renewal is crucial. How the pastor ministers and leads in the congregation after that, however, also requires new awareness and new sensitivity and new openness to *all* the people God gives to relate to. Not only the pastor but also the members of a growing church will seek to live by attitudes which truly reflect the fruits of the Spirit in fuller measure.

DISCUSSION

1. Ask the members of your class why they joined your church.
2. Examine Acts 2:41-48 as descriptive of the kind of internal climate discussed. What are some of the biblical characteristics of such a climate?
3. If the internal climate of a church is so important, are there any dangers in making an accepting and affirming climate an end in itself?
4. Share with the class a story or experience of how a congregation you know was revitalized.

Notes
[1] H. S. Bender, *These Are My People* (Scottdale: Herald Press, 1962), p. 88.
[2] Palmer Becker, "Here We Are, Lord" address to Canadian Conference (July 1978), p. 4.
3. Edward Kersten Perry, *Learnings About Fishing in Upper New York* (April 1975).

chapter 4

the importance
of group life

Church Growth Principle: *A growing church multiplies the number of meaningful groups in the congregation.*

Faith Mennonite Church, Newton, Kansas, has grown as a congregation from 104 in 1959 to 301 in 1979. One of the striking things about this congregation is the variety and number of active and meaningful groups it has for its size. I asked several persons from the congregation about the groups. Their answers were revealing.

What kinds of groups do you have in your church? There are Sunday school classes, interest groups, family cluster groups, Bible study-sharing-prayer groups, choirs, youth groups, ladies' groups, social groupings of couples, and interdenominational prayer groups. There is a total of thirty-five different groups which does not include the church council, the four boards, and several ongoing committees! Four years ago we placed a new priority upon sharing-study-prayer groups. Each year since then another one or two have been formed until this year the majority of the twelve home groups are such groups.

How do you get such a high level of participation in groups? Our groups themselves seem to be very interested in new persons who come. We also have two persons named from our Board of Witness and Outreach who are to watch for new persons and help them find their way into a group that would meet their needs. Our Sunday school, at the beginning of each Sunday school year, plans for a new class or two—there is a lot of flexibility. Our space is so limited at church we can hardly find more room. It's one of the reasons we're building a new wing now.

Each year in fall we also have an "Organizing Party" on a Sunday evening in September when Leonard Wiebe, our pastor, has focused on the value of groups in his morning sermon. That Sunday evening we re-form the small groups that meet in homes, though some of them choose to continue together as they were.

How many new groups have been formed in the last six months? Three—a young couples' Bible study and prayer group, a men's breakfast prayer group, and a family cluster group. The previous year we also had three new groups form.

Group life in many dimensions. While humanity in its sinfulness tends toward alienation and disruption of community, God's redemptive purpose is to create community as He brings us into fellowship with himself and with one another.

The church expresses community in many ways—by worshipping together, serving together, studying together, and helping one another. A typical congregation is not only one group, however, but many groups. Looking at the group life of a church is one good way of examining the quality of community being experienced there.

A congregation with a healthy group life is more likely to grow than a congregation which is largely a collection of individuals who may see each other only during the formal Sunday morning worship hour. Growth is further encouraged when more groups are formed so more people have a chance to be in groups in meaningful ways.

Formal and informal groups. Most congregations are really a variety of groups, some of which are formal and some informal. Most members "belong" to several of these groups at any given time.

Among the most common formal groups are groups like the church board, Sunday school classes, women's groups, youth fellowship, committees of various kinds, and the choirs. Some of these groups may be task-oriented, others study-oriented, others fellowship-oriented, although each may have elements of all three in its purpose.

Formal groups are called thus because they are organized and usually have a place in the organizational structure of the congregation. Informal groups are those which no one has organized and are not part of the official structure of the congregation. Examples of these groups are the five widows who sit in the same two pews together every Sunday morning, or the seven or eight young fellows who hang around together near the back door before and after church, the three couples from the large adult Sunday school class who go out together every Saturday night, and the men who go deer hunting at the same hunting camp each year. Such groups develop informally and usually fill some need for those who are part of them.

Usually informal groups are positive in their effects. They can, however, become cliques when they become exclusive. Informal groups can become divisive when they take on a purpose contrary to the purpose of the congregation, or when they see themselves as called to correct some things that are not "right" with the congregation, or when their concerns are not shared openly. Rumor, gossip, and underhanded ways are a hindrance to growth. Paul declares in 2 Corinthians 4:2 that he has renounced underhanded ways. We must also be open in our relationships to the whole congregation. Sometimes informal factions develop within a church, each rallying around certain causes or leaders in a divisive manner. The Corinthians to whom Paul wrote are a well-known biblical example of destructive factionalism in the church.

In a healthy, growing church both the formal and the informal groups are not only open to new persons, but also contribute to the accepting and affirming climate so important to a growing church.

Another way groups can be thought of is by size. Peter Wagner, in his book, *Your Church Can Grow*, suggests that we need to experience the church in three sizes—the large "assembly, the congregation, and the cell." The assembly is large enough that we don't know everyone personally. The congregation is small enough that we can know everyone by name and a little bit about them. The cell is a primary face-to-face group where we can get to know one another very well. We need to look at the various groups because our experience of the church is somewhat different in each of them.

The large assembly and corporate worship. In the large mass gathering we can be anonymous. It is not necessary, however, to know one another in order to enter into the experience. Our attention is largely focused up front where the leaders lead the meeting. If they are prepared, gifted, and skillful, and we have come with a genuine desire to worship, the experience can be a moving and worshipful one. Those who regularly worship with small congregations from week to week enjoy larger conference meetings which bring large groups together. The singing is inspiring, the music is uplifting, and the preaching challenges our minds and hearts. The whole experience feeds our souls in a way that no other experience could. It reminds us that God has made us part of a great family—a family brought together from every tribe and tongue and nation as pictured in Revelation 7.

It helps us in times of discouragement to know, as God reminded Elijah (1 Kings 19:18), that there are still many others of like faith! To be part of a large assembly enables us to know we can join hands with many brothers and sisters to do things in the work of the kingdom that none of us could do by ourselves.

The large public meeting and the Sunday morning worship hour, because of their image as public meetings, are also times when new persons feel free to visit. In North America our tradition of freedom of worship is still generally valued. Thus, in growing churches, the corporate worship experience is an important entry point for new people.

George R. Plagenz, Religion Editor for *The Cleveland Press* has been rating worship services according to how the service impresses him, how congregation members react, and what is keeping people away from the church. "A lot of people don't get anything out of church services and stay home" because of ineptly led services and poor preaching, he says.[1]

A study done by the Upper New York Synod of the Lutheran

Church in America, revealed that the worship hour in growing churches is exciting. It is well planned, moves, and holds attention. It showed that every congregation in growth trouble has something wrong with its worship life: it is boring or ineptly or slovenly done.[2]

Vital corporate worship. What is the key to a vital corporate worship experience? Is it better planned and professionally executed? These are important, to be sure, and some congregations have a worship committee which works closely with the pastor and the music leadership to plan well for corporate worship. But it is not showmanship we strive for! Worship is not entertainment. We can get that in other ways. If we want religious entertainment, an increasing number of religious television programs are being professionally done.

Is creativeness and innovation the key to a vital worship experience? Some congregations have worked hard to vary the worship experience to make it more interesting. But novelty itself is also not the key, as Dan Bauman points out in his book *All Originality Makes a Dull Church.*[3]

What is the key to a vital experience of worship? Acts 4:23-31 reports a vital worship experience in the New Testament church. The apostles had just been ordered to silence by the religious authorities in Jerusalem. Those who gathered to pray came with a deep sense of urgency and need. There was an air of expectancy. They came for a specific meeting with God. In verse 31 it is reported that the place was shaken and they were filled with the Holy Spirit and spoke with boldness.

Not all our times of coming together for worship have such an urgency about them. But in a vital corporate worship experience there is an air of expectancy. People have come to meet God! They are there because they expect to praise God; to join others in celebration of His goodness and grace; and to share the burden of a concern in prayer. They expect to be addressed by the Word of God proclaimed as good news, as instruction, as correction, as encouragement by a proclaimer who knows deeply whereof the Word speaks.

How is such a worship service conducted? There may be an "order of worship," but there is freedom to depart from it at any time. Merle Stoltzfus, pastor of a growing Mennonite church in Pennsylvania, says that he himself doesn't always know what their worship hour will include. There is opportunity for everyone to participate, not only in the singing and the litanies, but also with informal testimonies, sharing, and prayer.

The preaching of the Word is strong as an important element in vital corporate worship. There is no substitute for the personal communication of preaching. The Holy Spirit uses the well-prepared preacher who is willing to submit to the rigorous disciplines of preparation and effective communication. Whatever the style—whether it be a teaching style, a prophetic style, a low-key personal conversational style, or a confessional style—let it be one in which the Lord can use the preacher most authentically.

Growing churches have a vital worship experience that moves men and women at the level of the feelings and the will, as well as the intellect, so that their lives are changed.

The fellowship group. While new persons may first visit the Sunday morning service because it is conducted as a public meeting, they usually do not truly become part of the congregation as a community of faith unless they also become part of some group within the church where they can learn to know the other members of the group and experience a sense of belonging.

How large can such a group be? Some have suggested twenty-five; others up to 250. Lyle Schaller uses the term "fellowship circle" to refer to those who are part of the same first-name group in the church. In large churches, such groups as Sunday school classes or choirs, often become fellowship circles because they are small enough for members to know each other. The group itself has a name and purpose to help give it an identity.

The significant feature is that each member of this "intermediate size" group has a sense of belonging. Each will be missed if absent. There is time spent socializing as well as, for example, in Bible study (Sunday school class) or musical rehearsal (choir). Such groups often plan periodic social occasions such as dinners, picnics, or trips which encourage socializing. Openness of the intermediate-size fellowship group to new persons is crucial to growth of the congregation.

The importance of forming new groups. The formation of new groups is crucial to continuing growth. An experiment reported by Richard A. Myers, in "Sunday school, small groups and church growth," was conducted to find out if there is a relationship between the number of classes and growth of the Sunday school.[4] The ministers who participated in the experiment were divided evenly into two groups. The first group was instructed, "If a Sunday school teacher resigns this year, do not replace him or her. Instead, combine that class with another class of about the same age to make one larger class. Keep a close watch on the attendance and record what happens."

The second group of ministers was instructed, "In every children's department with two or more classes, add another teacher and another class. Then reassign the existing pupils to give all classes an equal enrollment. Monitor the attendance patterns of these classes for the coming year."

By the end of a year, attendance in every combined class of the first experimental group had declined noticeably, and was now no larger than it had been at the beginning of the experiment. In the second group, nearly all the classes which were divided had grown. Similar results were observed in adult classes. This experiment suggests that more groups mean more room for more people. Fewer groups mean less room and fewer people.

As fellowship groups grow they eventually become so large they stop growing. Continued growth depends on forming new groups. When is a group large enough to divide? Unfortunately there is no standard "right" size group. Different age groups mean different size groups. The younger the group, the smaller it needs to be. However, when attendance levels off in any group, it has likely reached its optimum size under present conditions. Personal fellowship between group members is more important in youth and adult groups than in younger groups. And the larger these groups become, the harder it is for people to know each other.

How can new groups be started? In youth and adult groups, arbitrary division of an existing group will cut across friendship ties, which hurts the whole effort. Instead, other ways need to be found. New groups might be started with people not currently in any group. Find someone who is really interested in forming such a new group. Appoint, train, and encourage that person to form a new group. Another way might be to form new Sunday school classes by asking existing classes to call on those who would be willing to lead out in forming a new class. They can be "sent" with the blessing of the existing class. They can thus multiply groups out of a sense of mission rather than feeling arbitrarily moved to a new group.

Certain age groups in the church are more open to the formation of new groups. Young couples and the cradle roll are the key ages at which new groups or classes are most likely to succeed.

The small group. The third level of vital group life which characterizes the growing congregation is the small group of twelve or fewer. It is often at this level that more personal caring and fellowship happen. The small group is known by many names today, for example, "cottage prayer group," "K-group," "discovery group," "home fellowship group," "seekers' group," or "growth group." Most of these groups meet about two hours each week in the homes of members. Each meeting usually includes Bible study, personal sharing, prayer, and informal socializing. Some groups may include training for some task. Some groups covenant together to keep certain daily spiritual disciplines and to pray for one another.

Such a group is small enough for every member to participate and to be known deeply by the rest of the group and, in turn, to learn to know the other group members more personally. It is the setting in which mutual burden bearing, sharing of personal joys, gift discernment, and prayer for one another are possible.

The small face-to-face group, like no other group in the church, gives us the opportunity to confess sins in our lives and experience God's forgiving grace. In *Life Together* Dietrich Bonhoeffer, a German theologian and pastor, writes, "The pious fellowship permits no one to be a sinner. So everybody must conceal his sin from himself and from the fellowship. We dare not be sinners. Many Christians are unthinkably horrified when a real sinner is suddenly discovered among the righteous. So we remain alone with our sin, living in lies and hypocrisy. The fact is we are sinners!"[5] But James 5:16 reminds us to confess one to another. In this way God uses our brothers and sisters in Christ to make the grace of the gospel real in our lives. When we experience forgiveness in our whole being, the joy of our salvation is renewed and deepened. The small face-to-face group is one of the most likely settings in which this happens.

We can also be held accountable for our commitments in the smaller group. Most of us hunger to be taken seriously as persons even though we may be uncomfortable at first with this aspect of a smaller group.

Smaller groups in the church are not new. Jesus began with a chosen group of twelve. Until the third century, the church itself was largely a small group movement, meeting in homes and multiplying around the Mediterranean world. Most of the letters in the New Testament are written to churches that met in houses. In later centuries, times of reform and renewal in the church usually included a new small group movement in the church. The class meetings organized by John Wesley were one of the keys to the strength of the Methodist movement. Renewal has not only come by way of a small group movement, but has often also been sustained and consolidated by small groups.

In the small group it is often possible to come closer to experiencing the church as a spiritual family. God has used the small groups of which I have been part to bring important changes to my life. It seems significant that young adults today who have grown up in an increasingly materialistic and fragmented world with its high rate of mobility, superficial passing relationships, and broken marriages, should often be most responsive to the opportunity to be a part of the small group. Those churches which encourage and plan for meaningful small groups will encourage growth.

What are the risks in starting more small groups? Some risks are involved as with any venture that may be new. Small groups can become isolated from the large congregation and become too sufficient unto themselves. Open communication and reporting to the large congregation helps groups relate to the rest of the congregation.

A common apprehension of some church leaders is that small groups encourage formation of cliques. Cliques, however, tend to form "spontaneously" rather than out of a planned program. Churches that encourage and plan for small groups are less likely to have cliques than those who do not. Annual or more frequent periodic review and/or reorganization of the small groups also help to keep them inclusive in spirit rather than exclusive.

One of the dangers of small groups is that they become so completely inward focused that they lose their openness to new persons. In a growing church the small groups are not only nurture and caring groups, but evangelistic as well. While the discussion and sharing and prayer are essentially nurturing to members within the group, these become evangelism as persons share this nurturing fellowship with those outside the churches. Persons in the group with the gift of evangelism will be sensitive to the readiness of new persons to make a personal commitment to Christ and help them with that.

As in other programs of the church, leadership training and support are important. It is often assumed that leadership is relatively unimportant in small groups because of the home setting, the informal structure, and the small size of the group. A commonly mistaken assumption is that everyone can be a leader, or that leadership should be passed around to give everyone a turn. One of the most common reasons for failure of a group to function helpfully is the failure to discern and identify leadership roles and gifts in the group. Ernest and Nancy Bormann, speaking out of extensive research in the functioning of small groups say, "The groups in which a leader failed to emerge were uniformly unsuccessful at their task and were, furthermore, socially punishing to their group members.

They were torn with strife, they wasted much time, and they frustrated the people in them."[6]

Small group leaders need orientation and training. Those who have never experienced the church as a personally caring fellowship will have great difficulty leading a small group, but they can learn. God has given every congregation those persons with the gifts that are needed. They can be given experience and training. An ongoing, supportive relationship with church and pastoral leadership helps them to learn from each other how to grow. This can be partially provided in regular meetings for sharing and mutual encouragement.

How can small groups be formed? Very often, congregations beginning with small face-to-face groups for sharing and prayer, find that they are, after all, much like the Sunday morning Sunday school class. There is more discussion of ideas as they do Bible study and more socializing, but little deeper sharing of themselves with one another. There may be an opening and/or closing prayer, but little ministry to one another in prayer. And the small groups begin to fade away as people continue in their familiar patterns of relating to one another. Just having a different time and place to meet will not make much difference. As soon as the novelty wears off, people lose interest unless something meaningful begins to happen that does not normally happen in the Sunday school class or other regular occasions for meeting.

The purpose of the Sunday school is Bible study. It has its own patterns. The purpose of the small groups is to learn to listen, to sense one another's needs, and to respond in caring ways. Different patterns and a different level of interaction prevail. The dynamics of a small caring group are quite different from that of the traditional adult Sunday school class. There is a growing sense of the Holy Spirit's presence as we are enabled to trust each other, affirm one another, empathize with one another, confront one another gently and lovingly when necessary, and be accountable as well as hold one another accountable in loving obedience to Christ.

When there has been no experience in the congregation with small groups, a small series of six or eight weeks with suggested guidelines may be a way to begin. Leaders must be carefully oriented. An evaluation should be held at the end. Do not be discouraged if not everyone participates. It has been suggested that about one-fourth of the people in the average congregation will enjoy this dimension of the church more than any other. But not all will be open to it.

There is no one best way to introduce the opportunity for deeper, more personal fellowship which small groups afford. Beginning with those who are ready and interested at first may be best. Whatever way is used, there are several elements groups need in a clear understanding of their group "contract."

First are the reasons why they want to meet and the expectations they have from the group. These should be discussed and agreed upon openly. Second is the general format—will there be Bible study, plenty of opportunity for sharing, time for prayer? Third is the leadership style, defining who is to lead and how. Fourth is agreeing on a meeting time, day of week, general length of meeting, and what is expected if you cannot attend a meeting. Fifth, the group may wish to find a way to encourage and hold one another accountable to some personal goals or spiritual growth disciplines. At the end of an agreed-upon period of time, the members need to reflect on their group experience to learn from it, evaluate it, and celebrate it.

A small group needs to go through a time of getting acquainted at the beginning. The leader can encourage this to happen helpfully. The way the leader functions in the group can either help or hinder the degree to which group members learn to trust one another. Judgmental attitudes kill the fellowship, while genuine unconditional positive regard for each other will encourage honesty.

Some congregations have found it helpful to schedule a special weekend renewal event like a Lay Witness Mission,[7] in which many have opportunity for meaningful small group sessions. This often becomes the beginning of new small groups.

Other congregations have found materials prepared by Faith at Work[8] or the Serendipity materials by Lyman

Coleman helpful in getting started. Mennonite Broadcasts, Inc., also offers a kit of materials for starting a small group fellowship.

In summary, a healthy and growing congregation is characterized by groups which offer a warm place of belonging and caring to every member of the fellowship. In such a congregation there are stable continuing groups that provide ongoing personal support to the individual members of the group and strength to the whole congregation. Growth comes not only through welcoming new persons to these existing groups, but also through forming new groups for new needs and for new persons who also need such a place of belonging in the larger body.

DISCUSSION
1. Examine Galatians 6:1-5. What are the marks of the community of faith according to this passage?
2. List the things you'd miss personally if you had no opportunity to be part of:
   A large assembly—

   An intermediate-size fellowship group—

   A small group—

3. Discuss the observation that new persons will not become part of the congregation nor remain active very long if they do join, unless they become part of a smaller group. Do you agree? Why is this true or not true?

Notes
[1] *Evangelical Newsletter* (July 14, 1978).
[2] Edward Kersten Perry, *Learnings About Fishing in Upper New York* (April 1975).
[3] Dan Bauman, *All Originality Makes a Dull Church* (Santa Ana, Calif.: Vision House, 1976).
[4] Richard A. Myers, "Sunday school, small groups and church growth," *Church Growth: America* (Sept.-Oct. 1978), pp. 8-9.

[5] Dietrich Bonhoeffer, *Life Together* (New York: Harper, 1954), p. 110.

[6] Ernest G. and Nancy C. Bormann, *Effective Small Group Communication,* Second Ed. (Minneapolis, Minn.: Burgess Publishing Co., 1976), p. 55.

[7] Lay Witness Mission (plans available from Institute for Church Renewal, Tucker, Georgia).

[8] Faith at Work, 11065 Little Patuxent Pkwy., Columbia, MD 21044.

the growing church reaches out

chapter 5

reaching out

Church Growth Principle: *A growing congregation has accepted evangelism as a basic responsibility of the local church.*

My wife and I came to the Alpha Mennonite Church with high anticipation—a three-year-old church, started "from scratch," now with sixty-plus members and steady expansion. I wondered what it would be like.

"We've arranged for you to eat out this evening with Lew Sabbatini," said Pastor Henry Swartley as we arrived. "I think you'll have a special evening."

It was unforgettable. A husky, intense brother of Italian descent, Lew hosted us royally from the start. Even before we reached the restaurant, he had opened his heart to us, and the evening was filled with conversation leading to close friendship. For us, the seafood dinner was a once-in-a-lifetime event.

Before dinner was served, Lew spotted a familiar face. "I think that waitress was a high school classmate," he said. He motioned her over, and engaged her in conversation. They had not seen each other for years.

She had indeed been a classmate, and before I was aware of what was happening, she was speaking of a recent nervous breakdown, and Lew was telling her how his life had been transformed by meeting

Jesus, and inviting her to consider the Christian way. I had never observed a more natural, winsome witness.

Later as I asked Pastor Swartley how new people are added to the church at Alpha, he smiled and said, "Well, there's Lew, and . . ."

Defining evangelism. Up to this point we have looked at the kind of church that grows because of what the church is like internally. Now we want to look at the growing church reaching out to people who are still outside the fellowship of Christ.

Evangelism as used in this chapter means to call persons to faith in Christ with a persuasive sharing of the gospel of Christ in deed and word in a holistic approach to people as persons. New Testament evangelism is what we might call incarnational evangelism—that is, evangelism that shares the gospel as Jesus did when He ministered on earth in the flesh, meeting people's needs, both temporal and eternal. Anything that helps other persons come closer to a saving faith in Christ strengthens evangelistic outreach. Thus, serving others expresses our faith in Christ in tangible ways: (1) It is the evangelism of presence. Much of the world will not be drawn to Christ nor believe without an authentic Christian presence. Helping others is essential to evangelism. (2) Evangelism is also proclamation. The good news must be articulated. The story must be told and Jesus must be clearly introduced in word as well as in deed. ". . . faith comes from hearing the message, and the message is heard through the word of Christ" (Rom. 10:17, NIV). (3) Evangelism involves persuasion. Our task is not complete only in sowing the seed. There is a harvest dimension to the task as well. (4) The goal of evangelism is incorporation into the visible body of Christ with nurture and training for participation in the ongoing mission of the church. The evangelized are not fully evangelized until they, in turn, become servants and evangelizers in the world!

Incarnational evangelism means that the congregation, as the body of Christ, will incarnate the Spirit of Christ as a healing and reconciling community of faith where new persons come to faith also.

55

Just as Jesus called persons to personal commitment, the church as the body of Christ calls for personal commitment to Christ as Lord and Savior. As Jesus ministered to the physical and emotional needs of persons, the church ministers to these needs. As Jesus confronted the authorities when they thwarted God's purpose and will, the church must not be afraid to confront the powers of this age. Incarnational evangelism means the church is reflecting the lordship of Christ with integrity in its life and outreach; not simply reflecting the prevailing attitudes and values of the times in which we live.

Evangelism in the early church, according to the account in Acts, was not carried out so much as a special program as it was an outgrowth of the Spirit of Christ at work through the church in many different kinds of experiences in the life of the church. Acts 2:42-47 suggests that evangelism flowed from the new fellowship experience. Acts 3:1—4:4 shows how evangelism happened around a healing event and the witness that followed. In Acts 5:1-11 discipline strengthened the church. Acts 6:1-7 suggests that further growth was encouraged by the way believers solved a problem in the church! They had confronted the authorities in Acts 5:17-42 and yet soon afterward many priests believed (6:7). Acts 8:4 tells us that they carried on evangelism as they were scattered by persecution, and Acts 8:6-8 links the hearing Philip received to his service ministry of healing. In Acts 8:26-39 evangelism happens as two men are traveling together. Dorcas, in Acts 9:36-42, is so beloved for her ministry as a seamstress that when she is restored to life many believe. The call to personal commitment in repentance and faith is heard again and again in relation to all these events.

The local church reaches out today. Evangelism happens in a local congregation today when outreach ministries are responsive to peoples' needs. Sometimes evangelism is spoken of in terms of meeting the needs of the church—for new members, for survival, for more financial resources, for the capable persons needed to carry on the church's many programs, for church growth. On various occasions I have heard expressed the hope that a certain new family would join because they would be "an asset to our church." But evangelism for the sake of the church as an institution tends to become imperialistic.

Outreach that is responsive to the needs of people will first of all try to identify, to understand, and to meet *their* needs. In an inner-city neighborhood, the needs of persons often seem very obvious, overwhelming, and difficult to meet, while middle-class persons do not seem as needy. Yet the needs of the more affluent are no less real, even though they may be less obvious in some ways. A mother on the poverty level often faces obvious material as well as emotional and spiritual needs. The middle-class suburban mother may also face anxieties such as the boredom of life without creative challenge, the lack of personal fulfillment in her affluent suburban lifestyle, or alienation in her significant relationships. Loneliness has been identified by researchers as the most prevalent felt need in North America. Loneliness is no respecter of race or class or economic status. Alienation and family breakdown are common among all classes of people. Sin has many faces of need.

A church that is sensitive to the needs of people will seek to identify and meet a felt need. For example, one congregation recognized how young mothers long for a break from the demands of caring for young children in the home day after day while husbands are away at work. So it developed a program called "Mother's Day Out." It provided care for the children and brought the mothers together for a good time of fellowship, special trips and outings, and some Bible study. A number of these mothers have made new commitments to Christ.

It cannot be overemphasized that when the church reaches out to meet human needs, we can respond to that need in some ways that a community agency or a government program does not. The church has the gospel to share, which meets human need at its core.

In recent years, for example, quite a number of churches have developed day-care programs for young children. Young families need a good place to leave their children while both parents are at work, or simply as an enriching experience for the children.

Lyle Schaller, a church consultant who works with hundreds of churches each year (from lecture notes, Feb. 1976, Pastors' Seminar, Associated Mennonite Biblical Seminary, Elkhart, IN), observes that churches operating weekday programs for children do so in one of two ways. Some of them see it as a service to the community. Others see it as a ministry of the church.

Operated as a service to the community, the children's weekday care program will usually not be seen as related to the life of the congregation. Little or no evangelism happens. If, on the other hand, such a program is considered a ministry of the church, it will be seen by the church as part of a larger package of ministries to young families and as part of the whole program and life of the congregation. This approach will be more likely to relate new families who use the weekday child-care service to the church itself. It becomes one of the entry points by which new persons are brought in touch with the gospel and into the congregation as they come to know Christ and the church.

Another example of finding a need and filling it with love and the gospel was shared by John Wimber out of his pastoral experience. He told of a young man in his church who had become aware of the many twelve- and thirteen-year-old boys in his neighborhood who had small motor bikes, but no place to ride them. Their fathers and mothers seemed to have more money than time to spend on their sons. The boys were too young to obtain the necessary license to ride their bikes on the street or public parking areas. This young man, with his pastor's permission and encouragement, arranged to take some of these boys to an area where they were able to ride. Being mechanically inclined, he helped them fix their bikes and keep them running. He won the boys' friendship, and some of the fathers began to get curious enough to come along and spend some Saturday afternoons with them. Several fathers, as well as sons, committed their lives to Christ and the church as this young man shared his faith with them around the Saturday evening campfire doggie roasts which became part of those Saturdays together.

How does one identify a need? By keeping our eyes and ears open. By getting to know people. By visiting and taking an interest in them. By praying for the Holy Spirit to make us aware of the needs that are there, and to help us to begin to see some possibilities for meeting them.

Sometimes the Holy Spirit opens the eyes of one person to a need and gives that person a "call" to respond to that need. When that happens, it should be tested and discerned clearly in the fellowship. If it is confirmed and further strengthened, it should be affirmed by the congregation so that those who see this need and hear it as a call in their own souls also may join in the active ministry to meet that need; and so that the rest of the congregation may be informed and be supportive of the venture.

Find a need and fill it. Evangelism happens as we respond to the Spirit's call to minister to the needs of persons, and as we remember that we have good news that meets the deepest need of all.

Evangelism happens when the members, as well as the pastor, learn to share their faith. James Kennedy maintains that the clergy-laity split which developed with the Constantinian era was the most serious blow to evangelism because it led to the attitude that evangelism is the pastor's job. He estimates that 95 percent of American church members have never personally led anyone to Christ. His answer is lay evangelism training. The congregation Kennedy serves developed a lay evangelism training program with great effectiveness. We cannot depend on such a program to do all our evangelism, but such training equips members to share their faith more effectively in their many other opportunities.[1]

1 Peter 3:15 reminds us that evangelism happens when the members of the body are ready to share in a gentle way at any time the reason for the hope that is within them. This means that an evangelistic congregation is one whose members are not only giving of themselves to reach others through the programs of the church, but also being witnesses in all their

various places in life. Someone has wisely remarked that we are witnessing all the time, whether we are aware of it or not. The question is, "What kind of witness are we making?"

Paul tells the Corinthian Christians, ". . . in whatever state each was called, there let him remain with God" (1 Cor. 7:24). David Schroeder explains that the Greek assumes something the English translation often fails to give us here. Schroeder points out that Paul is referring to the various stations in life that all of us have. One might be at the same time a son, a husband, a father, a teacher, a citizen, a motorist, and an engineer. Some of these stations are roles, some are occupations; some we have chosen, some we have not chosen; some are permanent, some are temporary. Each station has its obligations to others. What Paul is saying is that once we become Christians, we are to be Christian in all of our stations, and give testimony to the faith in each role.[2]

For evangelism, this presents tremendous possibilities. The New Testament church grew because Christians shared their faith in the various natural relationships they already had in their lives. Lyle Schaller reminds us that at least 85 percent of those who come into the church even now come because of relatives or friendship with someone in the congregation. The faith is still shared most effectively along the natural lines of relationships among people. The problem today is that our Christianity is often either so compromised to the spirit of the present age that there is no testimony, or it is so private that no one else is aware of our Christian commitment.

It has been demonstrated that as members learn to share their faith, evangelism happens because members sharing Christ are more like a satisfied customer telling another person why he likes a product, whereas the pastor is often seen as a "salesman" who shares the faith because it's his job! Members sharing their faith are like D. T. Niles once said of evangelism, "One beggar telling another where to find bread."

Such sharing of our faith happens best when those with whom we wish to share have learned to trust us as friends. This means making time for new people in our lives. Most of us already have a circle of friends and/or relatives. It is easiest simply to limit ourselves to those comfortable older friendships. We may need to pray and plan for ways to enlarge the circle of our own meaningful contacts to include new persons who are not Christians.

Christians sharing their faith need to be aware enough of their own sin to make "sinners" feel comfortable around them. Christians need to be enough in touch with their own humanity to help those who are different from ourselves to feel at home with us. One of the biggest obstacles to evangelism is the self-righteous holier-than-thou attitude Christians often seem to communicate—usually unbeknown to themselves. The Pharisees were bothered by the seeming ease with which Jesus moved among the despised "sinners, prostitutes, and tax agents" of His day. What was His secret? Certainly His way of relating to people reflected who He was—not self-righteous nor condemning, though He could be very confronting when that was the best way to express caring love. By His Holy Spirit He still seeks to give us the kind of openness and accepting attitude that treats other persons with loving respect and frees us from the fears we naturally have of allowing others to know us as we are. He frees us from the pretense and hypocrisy of "making a good impression." He frees us to be real—to express His caring love today.

Nine samples of local evangelism:

1. Ice Cream Evangelism—A pastor and wife, while serving a new church in Indiana, often fixed a freezer of homemade ice cream and invited new neighbors to share it and get acquainted. Some of these people later became part of the church there.

2. Drive-in Summer Sunday Evening Services—In Pennsylvania where the evenings are usually pleasant outdoors even when it's been a hot summer day, one church holds its Sunday evening worship outdoors in the parking lot! People come in their cars, stay in their cars if they like, or join those seated on the grass at the front. The program features outstanding musical groups and a message by the pastor. Cards with a word of welcome and opportunity to respond are distributed by the

ushers. Several new families come into the congregation each year through this "entry point."

3. Children—A weeknight children's Bible Club program held at the church each week by another congregation developed a wide appeal to the children of the community and provided the first contact for the church with many of the unchurched families in the community.

4. Visitation—Some growing churches have developed a regular program for visitation from the church by visitors who meet each week to visit and to share and pray with one another. Some of them use the Evangelism Explosion training plan to train visitors for sharing the gospel in their visiting. Some use other plans.

5. Pastoral Visitation—Some pastors give evangelistic visitation priority in their own ministry by setting personal goals like "visiting every home within a radius of eight blocks (or eight miles) of the church in the next two years," or "making at least three new visits each week," or "visiting each new person in the community within the first week of their arrival," or "sharing the gospel with at least one person not already part of the church each week."

6. Bible Study—In some congregations the home Bible study groups on Wednesday evenings are seen as an entry point for new people. While the content of the discussion will minister primarily to the growth needs of persons in the group, the gospel and the process of becoming a Christian are shared in some way (appropriate to the lesson) in each session. Certain Christians in the group may have the gift of sensing when a new person in the group is ready to make a personal surrender and commitment to Christ, and help the new person to take that step. When a group becomes too large it "commissions" some of its members to begin another group.

7. Mission Groups—The Church of the Savior at Washington, D.C., has developed a pattern of outreach through mission groups. Mission groups form as follows: (a) A member hears a call from God to minister in some way. Such a call may be to serve the children in a detention center, or young adults on a university campus, or the people in a large run-down

tenement house, or the single adults who may be living alone. (b) The member is encouraged to test the call in conversation and prayer with brothers and sisters. (c) If the call persists, the member is given a chance to sound the call before the whole congregation. (d) Others who also hear the same call in their own hearts are invited to join the first person to begin to pray and discern and plan how they might begin to work at their mission. (e) The new mission group, in its first meetings, also names the gifts represented in the group and agrees on who will carry which roles and responsibilities. (f) One-half of each weekly meeting thereafter is devoted to mutual caring and Bible study within the group and one-half to the business of the mission.[3]

8. Recreation—A congregation in Oregon discovered possibilities of using recreational activities such as softball, basketball, volleyball, bowling, and curling to meet and make new friends among the unchurched. This congregation sponsors a volleyball evening each week to which nonmembers may be invited.

9. Music—Another congregation plans and sponsors quality musical programs quarterly which are well advertised and draw into attendance persons who normally would not attend. A brief, well-prepared introduction to the church and its ministries and an invitation to return are given.

DISCUSSION

1. Do a quick survey of how evangelism happened in the early church. Note from each of the following passages in Acts what aspect of the church's life or what event seems to have had a direct evangelistic impact: e.g.,
   Acts 2:41—The Pentecost event and Peter's sermon to explain it.
   Acts 2:43-47—The apparently radical kind of caring fellowship and the impression it makes.
   Acts 4:4—
   Acts 5:12-15—
   Acts 6:1-7
   Acts 9:26-31—
   Acts 11:19-21—

2. What kinds of needs was the growing church in Acts meeting? See the passages you just examined.
3. Do you feel that every aspect of the life or program of the local church can have an evangelistic impact? How?

Notes

[1] James Kennedy, *Evangelism Explosion* (Wheaton, Ill.: Tyndale House, 1977), p. 4.

[2] David Schroeder, "Called to Proclaim the Gospel," *Biblical Perspectives of Church Growth* (unpublished papers presented at the Consultation on Church Growth, Bluffton College, Bluffton, Ohio, November 8-10, 1976), p. 6.

[3] Elizabeth O'Conner, *Call to Commitment* (New York: Harper and Row, 1976) and Gordon Cosby, *Handbook for Mission Groups* (Waco, Texas: Word, Inc., 1975).

chapter 6

leadership for growth

Church Growth Principle: *A growing church has leadership which encourages and enables growth.*

Out of a concern for improving pastoral care for the whole congregation, Pastor Larry Martens and his congregation began to seek a new pattern of leadership that God could use to bring greater health to their church.

"How does a body grow?" Larry replied, when I asked him about it, "Not automatically. It grows when there are leaders in the body who are growing and who are modeling the realities of the community of faith. I see the body growing, not because there is one super-leader, but as there is a growing number of leaders working together."

The increase of Koerner Heights Mennonite Brethren congregation in Newton, Kansas, from ninety in 1969 to 280 in 1978 is only one sign of its growth. Six months ago thirty-five of their members (including some key leaders) were commissioned to form a new congregation in Hesston. Six months later this daughter congregation had called a former Koerner Heights member as pastor and had grown to 125. Meanwhile, Koerner Heights itself had already received twenty-four new members. So the "mother" congregation, still overcrowded and growing, voted to plant another new church in the near future. But Larry is most excited about the way he sees persons, as part of the body, growing in their faith and in their own ministries through their enabling style of leadership.

"What kind of leadership are you talking about?" I asked Larry.

"I'm talking about a kind of leadership where we are mutually subordinate to one another. No one is at the top. The heart of our leadership plan is in our elders (couples) group. We decided to use the New Testament concept of elder because we wanted to underscore the fact that there are a number of spiritual leaders in a congregation. Each elder couple relates to a part of the congregation called a fellowship group. These fellowship groups meet at least once a month. I meet with the elders group twice a month. At our elders meeting we report on the needs in the congregation, we have instruction for our ministry as elders, share our own needs, and pray together. It is not a decision-making board," he emphasized. "We wanted to remain free from the usual business a board of deacons does. By now the elders do a lot of the spiritual ministry in the congregation. It's been freeing for me as pastor."

"Do you mean that you as pastor minister to the elder couples and they, in turn, to the congregation?" I asked.

"No. It's not like that. I am involved at any point in the congregation as needed. It's more like we're a team working and learning together."

"You're not saying it, Larry, but I am seeing that the kind of leadership you model as the pastor in the elders group and congregation is a very important element in this," I ventured.

"Yes, I think that's true," he admitted.

There is in every growing church a key person whom God is using to make it happen. Often the primary catalyst for growth in a local church is the pastor.

We may sometimes wonder whether the real secret of church growth is the pastor. Is it finally a matter of finding a pastor with "charisma"? Is what we really need a superstar pastor? Sometimes those of us who are not superstars feel our inadequacy more keenly when such pastors are held up as the models for us. The vast majority of pastors are not superstars, nor in situations that will attract national attention. God has called us to be faithful wherever we are. Only the Lord knows how many unheralded servants, both pastors and lay leaders, He has serving faithfully year after year in many, many unheard-of places. It is these men and women who also give leadership needed for the church to grow.

While the pastor does have a unique role in the growing church as we know it, much leadership work is also done by persons other than the pastor. This often goes unrecognized. As we discuss leadership we are not speaking only of the pastor. What can be said of the pastor must also be said of the lay leaders in the congregation. Thus, when we think of leadership for growth, we think of the pastor and the lay leaders in the congregation.

When asked what he considered a key factor in the growth of their congregation in the past twelve years, a pastor in Pennsylvania mentioned the attitude of his board members as the foremost factor. He said they emphasized a positive attitude that helps them to look for the possibilities. When a new idea is proposed, their first response is not, "We've never done it that way," or "We can't afford it," or "We can't do that," but it is more likely to be "Let's hear more about that," or "What are the possibilities in our situation?"

New Testament teaching about leadership. Jesus clearly emphasizes servanthood for those who will be leaders in His kingdom. In Matthew 23:1-12 He contrasts the attitudes and models of religious leaders in His day with the kind of leaders called for in the kingdom of God. He who would lead in the kingdom is called to be a servant of the rest, not exalted by a role to lord it over others, or to bask in the privileges of position.

Servanthood has sometimes, however, been misunderstood to mean a passive role. I do not believe Jesus means passive acquiescence. Servanthood means putting the lordship of Christ, the welfare of the group, and the mission of the church above self-interest. It means listening to the group, but not listening simply to follow the group. Leaders with the attitude of a servant are still leaders who lead!

Such a leader is a responsible person. The New Testament counsels leaders to remember the special responsibility they have before God because they are leaders (James 3:1; 1 Peter 5:1-5). Leaders will be called to give an account of their stewardship of the leadership responsibilities that were entrusted to them.

Such a leader is to be respected because of the work he or she does (1 Peter 5:5). The other side of that admonition is that they are so to lead as to gain the confidence and respect of those with whom they work.

1 Timothy 3:1-13 and Titus 1:5-9 underscore the importance of spiritual maturity for a leader. Ephesians 4 speaks of gifts fitting certain persons for certain leadership roles. In summary, the New Testament gives us a picture of a leader who leads rather than simply reacts, who is a trustworthy and responsible person, who is respected by those who know him/her, who is growing in spiritual maturity, and gifted for the task to which the congregation calls. Such a leader helps a congregation to grow.

Qualities of a growth leader. Because the most significant element in leadership for growth is the *kind of person* the leader is, rather than a set of *leadership methods,* we shall elaborate further on the qualities of the growth leader rather than on a set of leadership procedures. Of all the qualifications we might discuss in this chapter on leadership, I should like to underscore especially those which seem to be important to encouraging growth.

1. *A church leader has a genuine desire for growth.* We may have assumed that all church leaders desire growth. This is not always the case. In many congregations the leaders themselves are quite satisfied with things as they are. As the church becomes increasingly institutional and develops more and more interest in its own institutional maintenance, the desire of leaders seems to shift toward more control and protective self-maintenance rather than toward greater faithfulness in mission. An extreme example of this is church leaders who have openly insisted that the Great Commission was given to the twelve apostles and no longer applies to us. There may be no desire for growth because the whole experience of the leaders has been within a culturally and religiously closed group. They have no understanding of the kind of evangelism and outreach which could result in growth.

68

There are those leaders whose commitment is limited to other goals such as humility, separation, and simplicity, rather than to mission, and therefore they do not desire growth. God uses these commitments and may bless the witness of such congregations with growth. However, a leader who would give leadership for mission desires growth and hears God's missionary mandate to the church as central to its reason for existence in this world.

2. *A growth leader has faith.* The Scriptures speak of saving faith as a willingness to trust in Jesus Christ as Lord and Savior. Saving faith is given to all who desire it. The Scriptures also speak of faith as a spiritual gift (1 Cor. 12:9). This is the ability to see possibilities God is setting before us which many may not see. It means seeing a little farther down the road than the rest. The gift of faith is essential for growth leadership because one of the responsibilities of leaders is to hold before the group the vision God has for it. The gift of faith enables leaders to see that vision clearly enough to articulate it and keep pointing the group toward it. "Where there is no vision, the people perish" (Prov. 29:18, KJV). Leaders are keepers of the vision. The gift of faith means having a positive confidence that God is at work and can accomplish even more than we ask or think!

3. *A growth leader has love*—love for people, the ability to affirm people. Some churches have endured the critical and unloving spirit of their leadership and survived, but they have not grown. The preaching from the pulpit must not be negative and condemning in tone week after week. We have good news in Christ. Can that good news be articulated clearly so that hungry and burdened hearts can really hear it? The word of warning is needed, but leaders who can embody the Spirit of Christ in their attitudes toward people will help the congregations they lead to become centers of warmth and healing and wholeness and new courage.

A church in a large metropolitan area had gone through some very difficult years as its community changed from an all-white to an interracial community. Now it was one of the few truly interracial churches in the area. The spirit of love and caring for one another was evident in the meeting of the church board we attended there. The group was asked, "What factor would you consider most significant in the turnabout your church has experienced in the last six years?" Of the fifteen persons on the board, every one of them named the present pastor as the most significant factor. When asked why, they described him as one who was basically affirming and accepting in spirit. He had helped the gospel to come alive as the good news it is. While some pastors "harangue" their congregations about the racial and other social ills of the day, this congregation was learning in a new way what it meant to relate to each other as a part of the same family of God.

A steady diet of preaching that is designed to stir guilt in the hearers is neither prophetic nor pastoral nor helpful. A constant appeal to guilt becomes counterproductive because it eventually turns people to anger and resentment, rather than repentance and faith. Most of us talk a lot about love, but have far more to learn than we realize about what it means in our lives and relationships.

4. *A growth leader has the gift of administration.* Administration does not mean merely the paper work in an office. This gift is the ability to motivate and organize people to work together. It means the ability to lead in the shaping of goals and plans for the work. Once people understand what needs to be done, participation and cooperation is much better than when the goals are unclear and plans are not understood.

The inspiration of worship, the spiritual gifts, and Christian commitment itself need to be channeled into witness and service in the church's mission. This is the administrative task of leadership. This means drawing many people into participation, evoking the spiritual gifts for service, affirming and training more and more persons, and delegating responsibilities to others on the growing "team" of co-workers.

Gordon Cosby, pastor of the Church of the Savior in Washington, D.C., says the gift of administration is one of the most important to the church. In a growing church there are leaders with the gift of administration—either the pastor or persons with whom the pastor works closely.

5. *A growth leader keeps the leadership circle open to new persons.* Acts 6:1-6 illustrates what happened in the early church when a whole segment, new to the church, was not represented in its leadership. When the complaints began to surface around the distribution of bread to the widows, the apostles were open enough to the Holy Spirit to suggest the selection of additional new leaders from the ranks of the Hellenists who were up to now not represented. When the whole body was drawn into the leadership, we notice, according to verse 7, that the witness of the church went forth with new power and that blessing and new growth resulted!

The growth leader is part of a team, rather than a loner. The Apostle Paul nearly always worked as part of a team on his missionary travels. Even his letters are often written as "we" rather than "I." Growth leaders should not become prima donnas.

6. *Growth leaders are hard workers.* Being a leader in a growing church means rolling up your sleeves and pitching in. It means becoming personally involved in the outreach ministries. Giving lip serivce to evangelism, or even strong support, is not enough. While the pastor, for example, may not necessarily have the gift of evangelism, he is nonetheless to "do the work of an evangelist" (2 Tim. 4:5). It has been found that pastors who are not personally involved in the evangelistic ministries of the congregation find themselves slowly losing touch with the growing edge of the congregation, even though they are supportive of the outreach ministries. New persons being brought into the fellowship relate first to those through whom the Lord has reached them and touched their lives. If the pastor and at least some of the official board are not personally part of some of those programs, it becomes difficult either for growth to continue or for the current leaders to continue to lead. Effective outreach programs led by lay leaders without the pastor's involvement have sometimes outgrown the pastor and he has had to move on. More commonly, the growth of the congregation is slowed by the noninvolvement of the pastor or official board.

7. *A growth leader must have authenticity* communicated

by openness, honesty, and transparency of life with those served. We know and love the Apostle Paul so well, largely because he was so open about his own life, his own feelings, his own struggles, and his own faith in Christ. He knew that his ministry involved his whole person. He was able to say, "Imitate me as I follow Christ" (Phil. 3:17; 1 Cor. 4:15-17).

We have long emphasized the importance of a leader's whole life and example because the Christian life is as much caught as taught. Like it or not, after a number of years a group will more and more reflect its leadership!

But this has sometimes led us to assume that the leader must above all others be as nearly perfect in his conduct as possible. And those of us who are leaders in the church have often accepted this same expectation for ourselves. More and more we feel compelled to strive, at least, to appear above reproach! In fact, reading this chapter about the good qualities of the growth leader may have reinforced that feeling for some again! Perhaps you've been thinking privately, as you were reading this, "I'll certainly have to try harder because I don't measure up to all this!"

That's exactly the point! There is probably no one who has all the good qualities and gifts described here for a growth leader. Though it is clearly a continuing challenge, being a growth leader is not as far beyond the reach of most of us as we may think! It is not as much a matter of trying harder to be more perfect as it is a matter of becoming more vulnerable, more honest, more open, and more transparent persons as we relate to others and to God.

Authenticity is one of the key qualities because it relates to the way all the other qualities are freed for expression. Our affirmation of others, for example, becomes genuine rather than something we do because it is the right thing to do.

Authenticity means we are more clearly aware of our limitations as well as our strengths and our gifts. It means that we know we are not always just right! We can be more open to one another and less defensive. We can be more at ease deep within ourselves. We are being set free in our souls from the preoccupation with what others will think of us, so that we can be more truly present to others, and so that the love of Christ can be expressed and experienced more truly!

The quality of authenticity in a pastor means, for example, that the greatest gift he/she has to give is not a perfect example in conduct or all the right answers; but rather the honesty of his/her own search—not merely as a neutral sounding board, but as a willing witness for Jesus Christ. Such a pastor puts his/her own search and discoveries at the disposal of others. This means letting others get to know us as we are—without pretense and without apology. It means accepting the ministry of others to our needs—not expecting only to minister to theirs.

8. *A growth leader makes a long-term commitment.* It has been found that pastors of growing churches have longer terms of service than the average. This means they are committed to stay and to work with the congregation through the disillusionments that usually come after an initial "honeymoon" phase with a new pastor or a new congregation. This means being willing to work patiently to allow the kind of confidence and trust in one another to develop that comes only after a congregation works honestly and lovingly with a pastor through a variety of experiences both painful and joyful.

Leadership approaches for growth. There is one more question to be raised about growth leaders. Is there one approach to leadership to be learned and used as best? There are those who affirm any approach to leadership so long as it produces growth. But we also need to ask, What *kind* of growth results from each particular approach to leadership? Each leader's personality colors his/her functioning. Because people are different it can be expected that the personality of leaders will vary. This variety, provided it remains within the basic guidelines for Christian leadership—servanthood and the qualities of spiritual maturity—is part of the colorful variety that God has given His people. But the question of a leadership approach is different.

Not long ago I was riding in a plane with the national director of field services for a major farm organization. As he described the differences in attitude which he found among the people with whom he worked in different parts of the country, I was struck by what seemed to me an observable relationship between the leadership approach characteristic of the prevailing religious tradition and the attitudes of persons in those areas. Where their church tradition involved more authoritarian leadership, people seemed to have a rather fatalistic attitude about their own ability to effect changes in the world around them. Where the predominant church tradition involved a less authoritarian leadership, the people seemed more hopeful, and more willing to become involved in efforts to deal with problems and issues that needed to be changed.

If our goal is only numerical growth we could say that whatever approach brings most numerical growth is best, whether it be traditional, authoritarian, democratic, autocratic, charismatic, or whatever. Undoubtedly in large churches with an authoritarian leader some people have been reached who had not been reached for Christ before. However, since our goal is also to "teach new disciples to observe all things" it will mean encouraging growth in spiritual maturity as well. We will need to choose an approach which enables the members to grow in their participation, in responsible corporate and personal decision making, and in their own discipleship in everyday life.

Christians are to grow in their capacity to take responsibility. They are to mature beyond the stage of infancy and childhood in the faith when they merely accept and follow a leader without question, whoever he/she is. Leadership which does not encourage spiritual growth, whether it may produce growth in numbers or not, is not adequate.

I should like to recommend the enabler approach in leadership. Such a leader has already been described in this chapter under qualities of a growth leader.

What is an enabler approach? An enabler does not see his/her task as primarily "doing" the work of ministry, but as helping others to identify and carry out ministries which are uniquely theirs. An enabling leader will be quick to recognize and affirm new leaders. But recruitment of other persons is only half of the enabler's task. Consistent ongoing support and training are essential. Furthermore, the enabling leader has a learning attitude even as he or she teaches and trains others.

The enabler is free enough not only to affirm, but also lovingly to confront and to call for accountability in relationships. (See Gal. 2:11-14.) He or she is reliable, and inspires confidence and trust so that others can accept the honest caring confrontation that helps make relationships genuinely supportive.

Paul, in Romans 1:11, 12, writes, "I long to see you, that I may impart to you some spiritual gift to strengthen you, that is, that we may be mutually encouraged by each other's faith." The enabling leader emphasizes interdependence and genuine mutuality rather than making others more and more dependent on himself as leader.

Ephesians 4 clearly gives the purpose of leadership in the church as "the equipment of the saints, for the work of ministry" (verse 12). This becomes the test of our leadership— does it equip? Does it enable others? Does it train and build up the whole body for the mission to which God calls the church? Are the gifts of each one in the body being discerned, evoked, affirmed, and employed for service, witness, and worship?

Barnabas is not often thought of as a New Testament growth leader like Paul the missionary. Yet Barnabas was the first in Jerusalem to trust Paul and to introduce him to some of the other leaders (Acts 9:27). It was Barnabas who sought out Paul to bring him to the new church at Antioch as a teacher (Acts 11:25, 26). Barnabas had gifts that differed from Paul's. I picture him as a rather low-key, soft-spoken person who was easy to trust. He did not need to be up front. Yet he also seems to have been at the growing edge of the church at many points because he was himself an "encourager" (Acts 4:36) and enabler, and gave that kind of leadership!

The choice of an approach to leadership does not rest with the leader alone. The congregation has a major responsibility for deciding what approach to leadership it asks for and encourages. The enabling approach requires leaders with initiative and openness. It also requires congregations who participate actively and responsibly with their leaders. While a growth leader is often the key to growth in a church, the congregation, in turn, can do much to encourage and train leaders in an enabling style of leadership.

DISCUSSION

1. Examine the biblical passages referred to in this chapter to refresh your familiarity with the New Testament teachings on leadership. Do these passages suggest some principles for Christian leaders?
2. List those qualities and gifts which you would consider important for a growth leader. Because no one person embodies all of these, decide which of these you would consider most important for your church.
3. How can the members of a congregation help to encourage growth qualities in their leaders?
4. What kinds of opportunities does your congregation offer for people to gain leadership experience and training with support and supervision from experienced leaders?

chapter 7

dealing
with obstacles

Church Growth Principle: *A growing church faces and deals
with the obstacles to growth.*

There stood Jim Criswell, confessing his faith in Christ, ready for
baptism.

"But he's a member of the National Guard," thought Mark, a
member of the congregation. "If more people like Jim become
members at Mountain View, will it destroy our peace witness?"

The charter membership of Mountain View Mennonite Church in
Pennsylvania was composed of brothers and sisters who were
Mennonite by deep conviction and who had a sincere desire to reach
out in local evangelism. But Mark sometimes wondered whether
discipleship and evangelism were compatible.

"I'm willing to make adjustments for the sake of winning people to
Christ, but I certainly will not compromise my convictions. Take peace
and nonresistance, for example. I cannot change my stand for the
sake of church growth."

For months afterward, Jim Criswell periodically drove across the
mountain for National Guard duty, skipping church for the Guard. In
the meantime, the congregation's teaching on peace was never
minced, and yet Jim was fully received as a brother in the church.

Today Jim says, "If they'd have told me I had to leave the Guard that
morning when I asked for baptism, I'd have turned around, walked out,

and never returned. I'd have felt rejected, shut out. But these people loved me. Now I'm as deeply committed to the peace position of the Mennonite Church as anyone in the congregation. This is my church."

Why examine our obstacles. Howard A. Snyder suggests that church growth is not a matter of bringing to the church that which is necessary for growth, for if Christ is there, the seeds of growth are already present. Rather, church growth is a matter of removing the hindrances to growth.[1]

In this chapter we examine some of the obstacles to growth because identifying them helps us to become aware of them so we can begin to deal with them. We'll be more open to change when we recognize those things which are obstacles in our situation and understand why they are hindrances. Usually there are already strengths in every congregation. God is already seeking to move each group forward in its mission. To reduce the obstacles can free the group to use its strengths with greater effectiveness.

Spiritual renewal for growth often comes precisely at those points at which we realize our need to change and become open to it. The Bible calls that repentance. Repentance is a basic requisite to dealing with internal hindrances to growth. The areas in which we are changing can become our growing areas. Thus it can happen that facing and dealing honestly with our hindrances to growth becomes an important way of opening new possibilities for growth.

Even though each church must analyze its own hindrances, we can discuss some of the common hindrances to growth and suggest some possibilities for dealing with them.

External obstacles. Obstacles to growth are both external and internal. External obstacles have to do with the surrounding situation in which the church finds itself, such as a political system which is actively hostile to the Christian church. Opposition is an external obstacle. Persecution will slow numerical growth, but it can also purify the church and sharpen its perception and its communication of the gospel with new clarity and power! Acts 9:31 reminds us that after a time of persecution the church grew with new impact on its world.

2) *Unresponsiveness of people being evangelized is another obstacle.* Unresponsiveness may be rooted in affluence which lulls a people to spiritual indifference. Or it may be due to the resistance of people in a given area to the gospel. Their resistance may be caused by past experiences with the Christian church. Jewish people, for example, have endured centuries of anti-Semitic attitudes and mistreatment at the hands of "Christian" people. In North American communities longtime residents in a stable neighborhood are not as likely to be as responsive to Christian outreach as persons in a neighborhood with a higher rate of mobility.

How well do we understand the people around us? Paul said, "I have become all things to all men, that I might by all means save some" (1 Cor. 9:22). He sought to understand people and minister in ways that communicated to them.

Another set of obstacles has to do with the church building. Some church meetinghouses are almost hidden and very difficult for new persons to find. Fewer visitors will find us if our building is hard to find. A congregation can put up directional signs. Is the name of your church itself clearly visible, or has it become overgrown by shrubbery? Are the names of rooms or directions to various parts within our church building posted so new persons can find their way around? Those of us who are at home there know where everything is and sometimes forget that a new person does not.

Do people have difficulty finding a parking place? The persistent will find one in any case, perhaps. But it is those very persons whose interest is new and who are not likely to be persistent of whom we need to be mindful, lest some little thing like not being able to park their car discourage them.

Is your building getting too full? That puts an obvious limit on growth. Building larger facilities is one of the options we immediately think of. However, one church in Texas has formed three additional congregations as their place of worship got too crowded. They now have a Friday evening congregation, a Saturday evening congregation, and a Sunday evening congregation, as well as a Sunday morning congregation—all using the same church building. Another more common practice is to hold two services on Sunday morning. This, in effect, doubles the size of the building.

Inadequate size of the building becomes an obstacle to growth primarily when we allow it to. The obstacle lies in the way we value and use buildings. The early church had no church buildings at all during the first 150 years of its existence. People met in homes and various other places available to them. The movement spread along the many natural networks of contacts between people. One of the largest congregations in the world today, located in Seoul, Korea, can never all meet together in one building. As of 1976 it counted a membership of 46,000. It is a growing congregation of more than 2,600 house churches with two unpaid pastors in each house church and a staff of paid pastor-elders, each of whom is responsible to a certain number of house church pastor leaders. It continues to grow because it is not limited by a building.

Some common internal obstacles. Some common internal obstacles are strengths and yet obstacles. For example, a high percentage of family ties in a congregation means that larger extended families are serving the Lord together and we rejoice in that. But this can become an obstacle when it creates, in effect, a "closed" congregation into which it is difficult for new persons to enter except by marriage or physical birth.

Another such strength which can be an obstacle is a high percentage of longtime believers. This is good in the sense that members often have greater Christian maturity, but it becomes an obstacle when their Christian maturity creates a greater spiritual, emotional, and social distance from new believers, and isolates them completely from non-Christians.

Some congregations strongly emphasize separation and nonconformity to the world (2 Cor. 6:15, 17; 1 Cor. 5:9-11). This is a sound biblical emphasis, but for many it becomes an obstacle to outreach and growth because in their separation from the world they withdraw so completely from meaningful relationships with other people that they cut themselves off from opportunities for evangelistic witness. When separation becomes institutionalized in forms of dress, rules about cars, rules for farming, or other external aspects of daily life, the group develops a more and more unique culture of its own. This cuts members off even further from opportunity for evangelism—even though the principle of separation from the world is a genuine dimension of their devotion to God.

False assumptions as obstacles. While traditions can become obstacles when they cut us off from other people, certain false assumptions can also become serious internal obstacles.

One assumption which undermines evangelism and growth is the belief that *I have no business imposing my beliefs on anyone else.* Tolerance and respect for the personal rights of others has too often been ignored by the zealous, on the one hand, and misunderstood by the complacent on the other hand. Tolerance and respect for the rights of others are very important in how we go about evangelism, but never a reason for not doing it.

What may, in some cases, lie behind the use of tolerance as an excuse not to do evangelism are some mistaken beliefs about God. Beliefs that ignore the justice, holiness, and righteousness of God, for example, make His love little more than grandfatherly sentiment.

There are other assumptions which are not in the category of false doctrine, but which also inhibit growth. For example, the assumption that *the only solid growth is slow growth.* The book of Acts does not support this assumption. Whether growth is solid or not depends more on the quality of the teaching and nurture experienced by new believers than on the rate at which new believers are added to the fellowship.

With such statements as "the gate is narrow and the way is hard that leads to life, and those who find it are few," Jesus seems to suggest that response to the gospel will be small and growth will be slow. Actually, Jesus here calls for total commitment. It is costly to follow Him. It calls for a change of life as well as a profession of faith. We change slowly in life. Our resistance to the lordship of Christ in our lives appears and reappears in various ways even after we are believers. The longer we follow Christ, the more deeply He works the work of regeneration in our hearts and lives. That is costly; it is hard; but it is the way of joy and peace and of life eternal. Sometimes only few respond, but there have also been times when many have turned to the Lord. Numerical growth may seem to be rapid at such times. Yet compared to the billions without Christ, even those are few by comparison!

Sometimes there is an assumption that says, *"Growth cannot be planned; it is the work of the Holy Spirit,* and therefore spontaneous. After all, the Spirit is like the wind (John 3:8) and cannot be programmed."* We cannot manipulate the Holy Spirit. He is sovereign. But that does not eliminate Spirit-directed planning. To refuse to plan can be a way of avoiding commitment rather than a sign of greater faith. Expectant planning is a mark of faith that the Lord is at work building His church and we want to be committed and responsible participants in it.

Unresolved conflict. One of the most serious internal obstacles to growth is unresolved conflict in the congregation. A Presbyterian study was designed to identify more clearly the causes of growth or decline. Among other theories, participants tested the theory that churches heavily involved in social action declined in membership while those not so involved would grow. They found, however, that congregational involvement in social concerns was not as significant a factor as they had expected. But if the congregation experienced considerable *conflict* regarding this involvement, there was almost always a pattern of decline. Thus they suggest that the constructive handling of conflict in a congregation is more important to growth than involvement or noninvolvement in social action.[2]

Should it be our goal to eliminate conflict in the church? No. Conflict is one of the realities of life—even in the church. To eliminate it is probably impossible on this side of eternity. We often try to avoid dealing with conflict, but that leaves it simmering under the surface. One of the marks of faithfulness in a growing church is the kind of openness in the Spirit that allows conflict to be faced and dealt with. Learning to handle conflict constructively can itself be a witness to the unbelieving world as well as a freeing and growing experience for the believer. The obstacle of unresolved conflict is one the Holy Spirit can turn into reconciliation and renewal, turning an obstacle into an asset!

Fear. It is impossible in the scope of this chapter to discuss all the internal obstacles to growth, but one which is so common that it must be mentioned is fear. Leighton Ford, who for many years has worked with evangelism seminars and workshops, reports that by far the most common problem trainees reported was fear of how the other person would react.[3]

Fear is an obstacle. But it can also be a reminder that the results of sharing our faith are always in the hands of the Lord and we need to trust Him from beginning to end. If I ever get to the place where I have no inner trembling in sharing my faith, I know I would be tempted to begin to function more and more as if I could do it in my own strength. At the same time, if fear is blocking us, it has become a serious obstacle. We know that (as Paul reminded Timothy) "God did not give us a spirit of timidity but a spirit of power and love and of self-control" (2 Tim. 1:7). "Love casts out fear" (1 John 4:18). We need to help one another claim those promises more fully in our experience.

Is a name an obstacle? The name of a church, especially the denominational name, is one of the important elements in our sense of who we are. It is a label for our beliefs, our values, and what we stand for. It helps others to relate to us because they can feel they know who we are.

However, some have felt that a denominational name is an obstacle to growth. Groups such as Primitive Methodists, Dutch Reformed, or Mennonites are small enough not to be widely known or understood in the general population. The images outsiders have of such groups may often be erroneous. A common assumption among outsiders is that one must be born into them to become a part of them. Erroneous images and assumptions like that are obviously a hindrance if they cannot be corrected.

What is the answer? Some have suggested dropping or changing the name. But this may raise further questions. How is a name change to be made? Because of its deep association with our sense of identity, a name has strong emotional value and becomes very controversial. Much time and energy can be spent working through this issue.

If the question of name becomes a strong issue it may be revealing something else—either an inappropriate pride or a feeling of inferiority on our part! Some people may be embarrassed by their own name because they themselves don't know what it stands for. How we feel about our name is usually related to how we feel about ourselves. If we have a low self-image, we will feel apologetic about our name. A low self-image and apologetic attitude about who we are is clearly a hindrance to growth. The question of how we feel about ourselves is very important to our outreach. We do well to examine our feeling about ourselves—are we projecting our own self-image onto our name? It should be pointed out that a growing number of new persons have joined the Mennonite church in recent years because of what the Mennonite church stands for.

Will dropping or changing our name really facilitate greater outreach? Henry Brucks, executive secretary for the Canadian Mennonite Brethren board of evangelism, says, "I do not believe that the question of name will be a barrier to our outreach, as long as we hold to the central thrust of the gospel of Christ. Here on earth we will always have a label, whether it is Baptist, Alliance, Mennonite Brethren, or any other name. I think if we can become transparent, saying, 'Yes, we are Mennonite Brethren and here is our message,' then I think people will trust us enough to listen. By changing our name, we will not have changed our deeper characteristics."[4] The most important issue may not be the name, but whether others can get to know us, to trust us, and be accepted by us. What kind of meaning do we give the name by the way we relate to our neighbors?

How will a name change affect our theology over a period of years? Will changing our name speed the process whereby the world around us squeezes us into a mold of greater and greater conformity to the masses who have no special name to call their

84

own among the people of the world? Our name helps to keep us in touch with our own history. What happens to a people which loses a sense of its own history?

Obviously promoting our own name is not our goal. Promoting the name of Christ is. Are there ways that our unique name can strengthen our witness to what the lordship of Christ really means in the church?

When a new church chooses its name it seems to be faced with two choices. One choice would be to choose a name that identifies with the community and says, "We want to serve our neighbors." An example of this kind of name might be "Maplewood Community Church." The other choice seems to be to select a name that emphasizes who we are, such as "Faith Mennonite Church," and says, "Come to us; you are welcome." Perhaps a combination of these two choices might be a third choice that would say both! New people do want to know who we are. We do well to be open and "up front" about it, while clearly and honestly reaching out to them in love.

One pastor of a Mennonite church shared with me how he had learned to move beyond an apologetic attitude as well as beyond a "pushing" attitude about the Mennonite church as he shared the gospel. If a new person with whom he was visiting asked, "Mennonites? Who are they?" he had learned to give a simple, direct, and positive answer that quickly summarized some of the basic elements in his peace church heritage. It went somewhat as follows: "We represent a church that has long believed in nonviolence in all situations, in living by a simpler lifestyle that conserves natural resources, and in helping one another in practical ways. Some pictures you have of us probably show how some of us try to live out those beliefs. Recent events in our world have underscored the wisdom of these beliefs in new ways. May I share how that became meaningful to me?" Most of the time the questioner is not interested in a long answer. Sometimes such questions are diversionary like the Samaritan woman asking Jesus where was the right place to worship when the conversation moved toward her embarrassing domestic affairs. A short positive answer avoids getting sidetracked from your purpose to relate to their needs and to keep Christ central in your sharing with them. To share who we are in a positive unapologetic way can even begin to turn what we sometimes see as an obstacle into an asset!

"Obstacles" to growth which should not be changed. The gospel, from the beginning, has been offensive to some. Facing obstacles to growth does not mean trying to remove all those things which might be an offense. Paul sought to be honest and straightforward in sharing the gospel, allowing the truth and power of the gospel itself to speak. The early church was not a popular movement in its time, but it spread and grew nonetheless. While we remind ourselves that we are not to offend others needlessly, our goal is not popularity, but faithfulness to Christ.

Some of the things which appear to be obstacles we accept as a part of our faithfulness to Christ. These we do not attempt to change or remove even for the sake of growth. Paul writes of this in 1 Corinthians when he says, ". . . we preach Christ crucified, a *stumbling block* to Jews and *folly* to Gentiles . . . I decided to know nothing among you except Jesus Christ and him crucified" (1 Cor. 1:23; 2:2). The essence of the gospel and its basic implications cannot be compromised. But it is not always easy to decide how much should be included in the essence of the gospel—especially as we begin to spell out the ethical implications that are inherent in the message itself. The gospel is clearly good news of God's grace toward us in Jesus— His life, His ministry, His death, and His resurrection. By His atonement we are saved by faith and live by obedient faith that continues to be sustained by the amazing grace of our God! Our new life is born by grace and continues by grace.

But the gospel has always had ethical implications for us from the moment we exercise saving faith. It cannot be proclaimed without them. Every Christian evangelist in the history of the church has selected those particular ethical implications he or she considered primary. Not only faith but also repentance is essential for true conversion. Faith is trusting God because He alone is completely trustworthy. Repentance is the turning away from the sin of trusting other gods to trust in God. Every evangelist has helped us see how we have expressed our trust in those other gods as the gospel has been proclaimed so that there could be repentance and faith with biblical understanding. It is in the living of our lives, in the choices we make, and in the values we live by that we show which gods we actually trust. Just as our obedience to Christ reveals the genuineness of our faith in Him, the "gospel" we live reveals the gospel we really believe. The gospel we live either validates or invalidates the gospel we proclaim. Thus the gospel of Jesus cannot be compromised in its message or in its implications, both out of our reverence for Him as Lord, and for the sake of the world He seeks to win through our witness!

A Presbyterian study tested the theory that churches which consciously stand apart from their surrounding culture in the values they emphasize will grow more than churches which identify with that culture. It was found that the congregations which grew the most numerically reported greater similarities with their surrounding communities, their lifestyles, and their values.[5]

A Gallup poll conducted in 1978 to probe the values, interests, and backgrounds of the unchurched in the United States showed that the unchurched differed very little from the churched in their values. Only on the question of abortion and sexual morality did the unchurched differ markedly from the churched. Sixty-one percent of the unchurched, but only 39 percent of the churched, for example, agreed that a married woman should be able to obtain a legal abortion.[6] Surely the values of the kingdom of God are not so similar to those of our world that there is no more difference than that!

These studies suggest that the implications of the gospel which are emphasized in many churches do not challenge the prevailing generally accepted *ethical* belief system of society at large except in selected areas of sexual morality. To challenge the belief systems of nationalism, militarism, materialism, and racism with the claims of the kingdom lifestyle that should be the fruit of the gospel could mean a far greater distinction between the church and its surrounding culture. For example, during wartime when our churches chose to emphasize faithfully the kingdom teaching against war so that our members actively sought alternatives to participating in the war effort, they sometimes became so unpopular in their communities that they did not grow very much numerically in those years. However, later a growing number of younger people were drawn to the Mennonite church because it stood against participation in war even when it was unpopular to do so.

It is my observation that rapidly growing churches too seldom challenge the prevailing belief system of the larger community except in selected areas of personal behavior. To deal only with certain kinds of personal behavior actually fits the underlying prevailing belief system of our society in that society values individualism highly. But our Lord's call to make disciples means we call others into new community and in that community we are to learn to "observe all things I have commanded you." If we compromise too many of those teachings for the sake of growth, we may find in the long run that we have sold our birthright in the gospel for a mess of American civil religious pottage which blesses the military establishment, defends our materialistic way of life, and promotes the satisfaction of self as the good life. Thus there are some obstacles to numerical growth which, to remove them, would be unfaithful to Christ as Lord.

Discerning between the obstacles we must not remove and those we should seek to remove requires wisdom, courage, prayer, diligent study of the Word, and openness to the Holy Spirit's leading. We may discover that the real obstacle related to unpopular ethical implications of the gospel, such as our Christian peace teachings, may be mostly in our own attitude. We become apologetic. We lose our own courage to share what may be unpopular. Or, at the other extreme, we become very defensive and argumentative in our attitude. Such an attitude tends to deny the truth we may be trying to promote!

While this dimension of the lordship of Christ may slow the numerical growth of a congregation which seeks to be faithful to "teach *all* things," let us also remember that the Lord is already at work preparing hearts to hear. After a consultation on church growth in November 1976, John Wimber, a speaker from the Institute of American Church Growth, reminded the audience that there are millions of young adults in North America who, since the Vietnam era, have a new openness to hearing about the peace implications of the gospel as peace churches can credibly share them today. To follow Jesus in faith will challenge the faith our society puts in its armed force. It will still be difficult, but this may well be one of the most basic faith issues of our time.

Some of the tension we have felt between faithfulness to Christ as Lord in all things and wanting to share the gospel winsomely will probably continue. It seems to be in the very nature of our task of reaching out to "win" others to Christ. It will never be something we accomplish in our own strength. We can appreciate Jesus' counsel to "be harmless as doves and wise as serpents." We rejoice in His promise "All authority is given to me . . . lo, I am with you at all times!" Let us continue to seek the Holy Spirit's leading as we learn to share the gospel with integrity and love; and trust Him to bring the repentance and faith God desires!

DISCUSSION

1. Read 1 Corinthians 1:18—2:5. Why did Paul not change his message even though the gospel was a "stumbling block" to the Jews and "folly" to the Gentiles?
2. Discuss with the class obstacles to growth you don't understand.
3. Howard Snyder, *Church Growth and the Kingdom* (p. 119), describes the following as obstacles to growth: spiritual disunity, immorality, false doctrine, unbiblical traditions, rigid institutional structures, clergy-laity dichotomy, edifice complex, rigid denominational structures, and sterile worship patterns. You may either wish to develop your own list or discuss the ones Snyder names which you see in your own situation.

Notes
[1]Howard A. Snyder, The Community of the King (Downers Grove, Ill.: Inter-Varsity Press, 1977), p. 119.
[2]Reported in *Action Information,* Vol. 2, No. 3 (September 1976), published by Alban Institute, Inc., Mt. St. Alban, Washington, D.C.

[3] Leighton Ford, *Good News Is for Sharing* (Elgin, Ill.: David C. Cook Publ. Co., 1977), p. 15.

[4] *Mennonite Brethren Herald* (October 27, 1978), p. 2.

[5] Reported in *Action Information*, Vol. 2, No. 3 (September 1976), published by Alban Institute, Inc., Mt. St. Alban, Washington, D.C.

[6] Reported in "The 'Unchurched': Who and Why?" *NCCC Chronicles,* Vol. 78, No. 3 (Fall issue), p. 1.

chapter 8

growth by church planting

Church Growth Principle: *A growing congregation intentionally plants new churches.*

What sparks the desire of a congregation to sponsor a new daughter church? Pastor Kenneth Bauman remembers how the Lay Witness Mission in the summer of 1975 brought new openness to the Spirit of God in his congregation. It began a new outreach training program, which later became important to its new church-planting venture.

In November of 1976, Kenneth and a number of leaders from the congregation attended the Church Growth Consultation in Bluffton. In a conversation with Peter Wagner and John Wimber the suggestion was made, "Your congregation at Berne could plant a new church every five years!"

That suggestion was taken home, prayed about, and acted on. The Board of Deacons came to the congregation with a proposal that a new church be planted. It was adopted. Next, the board carefully selected, and the congregation confirmed, a new church-planting committee. It checked with the Central District minister and the mission committee about possibilities. At this point they learned of Fair Haven, a struggling urban congregation in Fort Wayne. They assisted Fair Haven for about a year until it was on its own.

Meanwhile the church-planting committee continued exploring further needs for planting a new church. A resource person from the

General Conference office at Newton for a Church Planting Seminar met with the committee and the advisory council of the congregation. This helped them outline their strategy. They have now taken decisive steps to sponsor a completely new congregation. They have called a church-planting pastor, chosen an excellent location in fast-growing suburban southwest Fort Wayne, and have begun to gather a new congregation there.

Growing churches expect to "have children." Until now we have focused on internal growth from within the congregation and expansion growth that results from congregations reaching out. In this chapter we look at extension growth which comes with starting new churches.

New churches have begun in many different ways. Church planting is one of those ways. Church planting means that someone, some congregation, or some agency has intentionally started a new church. The ministry of the Apostle Paul described in Acts and reflected in his epistles was a church-planting ministry. Those new churches did not simply emerge and develop on their own. There is considerable variety in the ways those early church fellowships got started. Some began with a nucleus from the local synagogue which responded to Paul's ministry; others began in homes with a family or household. One of them began when Paul joined a prayer meeting of devout women at the riverside. They were intentionally planted through the initiative of Paul, the missionary, and his team.

The growth of the whole church depends on intentional planting of new churches, whatever strategy or plan is used. Dr. George Hunter, Executive for Evangelism for the United Methodist Board of Discipleship, points out that one of the major reasons for the numerical decline of the United Methodist Church in the last ten years is the fact that it has averaged only twenty-five new churches per year, which was fewer than the number closed each year.[1]

Church planting itself has taken many forms. Some churches have their beginning through the ministry of one person or one family. The story is told of a truck driver who decided to offer himself and his house as the beginning of a new church. He put up a sign at the end of his street.

Baptist Church
1937 Vine Drive
———→

One day another man stopped at the house to inquire about the church.

"You mean this is it?" the visitor asked.

"Are you interested in a church?" the truck driver asked in return.

"Why, yes, that's why I stopped."

"Well, then, that makes two of us—and that's enough for a church!"

With that beginning, a new fellowship grew in the truck driver's house, and in the next eight years five more congregations were planted from the initiative of that new congregation.

In a Mennonite church, a layman, after his conversion, discovered he had the gift of evangelism. After a few years, he felt called to plant a new church. He sought the counsel and blessing of his congregation, and it affirmed him in his call. So he left his good job with a major utility company, and sold their home. With cash enough to live for three years, he and his wife moved with their three children to a nearby city. They believed that the Lord could gather a new self-supporting congregation in three years. At last report, nine months after they arrived in their new community with only their family, they were a fellowship of eighty believers!

A new fellowship often emerges around the ministry of a missioner who has either been sent or has gone into a new area in a tent-making ministry (from the Apostle Paul's practice of supporting himself with tent-making while he ministered and travelled) on his or her own. One such missioner who has planted four new churches explained his strategy. He looks for a key family of committed Christians living in the area, interested in evangelism, and willing to open their home to gathering a fellowship. He calls them his "seed family." Then they begin to advertize in local papers and contact neighbors.

Henry Swartley, a pastor in New Jersey, has led in the planting of several new congregations—all within driving distance of his home. He advises, "Keep the organizational part of it as simple as possible. Let it grow out of the needs of the group itself. Keep emphasizing the basics and trust the Lord to build a caring fellowship."

A number of new congregations in each generation have emerged out of small groups of like-minded individuals and families being led of God to band together in a congregational covenant. They may seek a relationship with one or more denominational bodies or remain organizationally independent.

Denominational sponsorship. In earlier generations the Methodists had their circuit-riding ministers and Mennonites had their "Reiseprediger" (traveling preachers) whose ministry was designed to gather new groups of believers. They were usually sent by the conference of already established churches. Many of the groups established in this way became growing congregations.

The approach to planting new churches through denominational or conference action and sponsorship is another way that has been widely used in this century. Home mission boards and committees have emerged essentially as church-planting committees. Through such committees the other congregations in the denominational fellowship offer leadership, counsel, and financial subsidy to new congregations. They may call and send a missioner into an area to begin to gather a new fellowship, as well as affirm and assist an already emerging new fellowship which desires a relationship with other churches in this way.

It has been demonstrated that the goals that denominations are willing to set for themselves in church planting make a difference. For example, the Southern Baptist Convention of South Texas set a goal of 100 new churches in 1975. It started 138. In 1976 it set a goal of 150 and started 189. The Mennonite Church, during the 1940s and 1950s emphasized that every congregation should have a mission outpost. That became a time of many new church plantings.

The selection of a missioner with the gifts for church planting seems to be the most significant factor in the success or failure of any new church-planting venture, all other things being equal. The Baptist Convention in Ontario has a church-planting strategy that recognizes the key role of the leader. When it determines an area with need and potential for a new Baptist congregation, it calls an experienced pastor who has demonstrated that he has the evangelistic and pastoral gifts needed for the task. This pastor is given financial support equal to the support he would receive in any larger congregations. It is estimated that in five years, with this strategy, a congregation can emerge which will be financially self-supporting. It is working very much as expected.

Guidelines for denominational church planting. There are a number of helpful guidelines growing out of denominational church-planting experience which we do well to consider.

1. New churches may need a beginning nucleus of committed families interested in their denomination, but new churches do not grow by gathering persons of the same denominational background. They grow by winning people to Christ.

2. The effects of financial subsidy to new churches should be carefully monitored. It has been suggested that new churches should be off denominational subsidy in three to not more than ten years. After that other options like a tent-making ministry may need to be considered. New churches can be hindered in their growth by too much outside money, as well as by too little. A schedule of diminishing denominational subsidy is essential to avoid developing a pattern of dependency. Subsidy can be extended, if necessary, more easily than it can be shortened.

3. A regular meeting place should be selected as early as possible. A regular place and time of meeting strengthens the sense of stability and encourages growth. Place changes and frequent time changes make it much more difficult for new people to gain access to a group.

4. Selection of a name for the group should be done as early as possible for two reasons. First, a name is very helpful to the forming of an identity for the group. Secondly, to wait until the group becomes larger will usually result in a name becoming

attached by common usage rather than thoughtful choice. Choosing a different name later in a large group usually becomes controversial. It will mean "unlearning" an old name in order to use a new name. And because the name is so closely linked to identity, the new name opens the question of identity in "midstream"—at least in the feelings of people where the significance of identity is most crucial. As we have noted earlier, a clear sense of identity is an important factor for growth.

5. Avoid multi-denominational new church planting. The reasons for this are as follows: accountability between sponsoring denomination and the new church group is difficult to establish and maintain. The pastor may be accepted in the several sponsoring conferences, but be nowhere accountable. Identity for the new group becomes considerably more difficult to establish clearly. The differing polity of the various cooperating denominations can require an inordinate amount of time and energy in the new congregation around organizational procedures. Further, to maintain a meaningful relationship with several denominational bodies takes precious time and energy which the new congregation needs for its own mission. There are few such new multidenominational congregations that have grown. When they have, denominational identity and relationships have been treated as secondary as members "pick and choose" among the many denominational obligations and resources available to them. Inter-Mennonite churches may be an exception because they are more like various members of the same denominational family.

6. If there are plans to build a building, site selection should be done as early as possible. Land costs keep rising during an inflationary period and choice locations will not long be available. If a site later proves unsuitable, it can be sold in favor of another selection.

7. Select pastoral leadership carefully and aim for long tenure. The continuity which long tenure provides is important to a new group. One exception to long tenure might occur when leadership style needs to change to allow for continued

growth and the pastor is not able to change his or her style of leadership. Lyle Schaller suggests that a pastor's leadership style needs to change by the time a congregation reaches fifty or so in size. A style where the pastor takes on most of the leadership will tend to keep the church small enough for one person's leadership. A pastor who can learn an enabler and supervisory style will affirm, train, and share leadership. This style encourages continuing growth.

8. Keep organization simple. Let it grow out of local need rather than trying to have all the organizations of older, larger congregations.

9. Focus on mission purpose, set goals for mission, train for mission, and develop mission ministries.

Daughter congregations. Another way of church planting, older than denominational sponsorship in church history, is the planting of new churches by congregations. These daughter congregations are either started by someone sent by the local congregation or by a group of the members from the sponsoring congregation, or both.

While each situation is somewhat unique, this process can be planned and carried out in an orderly, step-by-step manner. Each congregation needs to design a plan for its own situation. The following is one example:

1. Assess the health and readiness of the sponsoring congregation. Prepare and strengthen the sponsoring congregation through teaching, prayer, discussion, and study for the prospect of parenthood. As long as a sponsoring congregation sees the commissioning of some of its members to begin a new church primarily as a loss to itself, there is not likely to be the necessary desire to move forward. If the sponsoring church itself is a growing church, it is more likely to see sponsoring a daughter church positively.

2. A sponsoring congregation may wish to decide when it is "big enough," after which it needs to commission part of its membership to begin a new church. What is an optimum size for one congregation? There probably is no "ideal size," but we do need to seek the Lord's leading in what He calls us to be and do, and where to go. The larger congregation is better able to

97

develop a wide variety of ministries to a greater variety of needs. The smaller congregation has other advantages, such as greater intimacy of fellowship, and more opportunity for everyone to participate actively.

The important point is that each congregation be willing to plan thoughtfully and prayerfully, in the light of its own situation, what its goals should be. A growing congregation can decide at what size it will plan to sponsor a daughter congregation rather than simply continue to grow larger indefinitely.

3. The sponsoring congregation can give leadership to the move to plant a new church. It can do this by appointing a new church committee and adding to its own staff a minister of extension whose task it would be to help get a new group started.

4. Even after the new group is formed, there can be certain strengths for the new group in the close relationship it has with the sponsoring congregation. Youth from both new and sponsoring churches can be part of one youth fellowship. The pastoral staff of both churches can be available for special ministries in both groups. The leadership training available in the sponsoring congregation can be used by the new church. All of this assumes the new church will be within reasonable driving distance from the sponsoring church though far enough away to serve a different area.

5. Financial responsibility for its own needs can be transferred to the new group according to an agreed upon schedule as it is able to assume this responsibility.

A sponsoring congregation at too great a distance from the daughter congregation to have member involvement in it finds itself in a somewhat different situation. Nevertheless, the congregation-to-congregation relationship—even at a great geographical distance—has reasons to commend it as a way God can use to multiply churches. The more personalized relationship between two churches can itself greatly enhance the process.

Daughter churches are sometimes planted through church splits. Some of these separations come about amicably, but most are the result of unresolved conflict. Church planting like this has been dubbed "unplanned parenthood." If the resulting new groups can leave behind them the contentious spirit which often characterizes such situations, each of them may begin to refocus its attention and energy on the mission of the church and grow. However, it is not uncommon for "splinter groups" to splinter again and again. The spirit of strife sometimes hangs on to hinder growth.

What kind of new church do we want to plant? Is there a New Testament model which we must keep in mind as we work toward the planting of new churches? There has been considerable discussion of what constitutes the best pattern for new churches. The term *sanctuary model* has been used to refer to congregations whose goal is to become a congregation large enough to support at least one pastor and to have a sanctuary large enough for the whole congregation to meet together every week for worship. This is the most common model in North America. The term *house church model* has been used to refer to a congregation small enough to fit into an average home so that all its meetings would be in a home setting, where participation and fellowship could be more personal and leadership more informal. The term *assembly model* refers to a congregation made up of two or more house churches which assemble periodically, yet which have the primary focus of congregational life in the house church.

Any of the above models can be faithful expressions of the body of Christ. As we have noted earlier in Chapters I-IV, any large congregation needs to include all the dimensions of fellowship—large, intermediate, small group; and to reach out, as well as to "teach all things." The house church also needs to reach out as well as to nurture the spiritual life and commitment of its members. If it does, it also may grow. The choice for the house church then may be to shift to a sanctuary model or to form additional house churches with or without the assembly dimension. Many sanctuary model congregations today once began as house-church-size groups. The assembly model, as may be seen in one of the largest congregations in the world (located in Seoul, Korea) has a structure that can be very

99

open to growth. (See Chapter VII, page 80.) The single house church, however, faces a strong tendency to become inward focused and locked into no-growth patterns.

In summary, it must be emphasized that patterns or models are not the most important issue. They may vary from place to place and from time to time. The more important question is whether or not we are a church in which the basic biblical principles for the church are evident. The church is a fellowship of believers in which principles such as love, faith, hope, and peace prevail. Sometimes these principles are stated in terms such as nonresistant love, mutual caring, simple living, honesty, stewardship, and worship, but all of them are rooted in the gospel of grace which brought us into being as a church.

Patterns and models are often culturally related and vary from place to place. When we try to copy patterns and insist on certain models, we may find they do not always fit or work. We may too often have gotten locked into certain patterns in our past church-planting endeavors because we confused patterns with principles. Thus it must be emphasized again that Christ is the living Lord of the Church and that by the Holy Spirit He continues to draw all men to Himself. He continues to teach us new things and to lead us into all truth as we need it for our own time and setting.

What about declining congregations in rural areas? In a chapter on growth by multiplication, it may seem inappropriate to discuss the closing of churches. But churches do cease to exist. Usually there are four choices when congregations decline. They may simply do nothing and disappear—that is, everyone finally moves away or dies. Or they may choose to disband at some point because it is no longer considered feasible to continue as an organized fellowship. They may decide to relocate in a nearby town or city. Or they may decide to merge with a sister congregation of the same denomination or neighboring congregation of another denomination. There may be still other options. Some rural churches experience years of decline and finally face a choice. It is important to make a choice rather than just drift into one unconsciously.

100

The following questions are raised for such congregations to consider:

1. Why does our church continue to be important to us? The size of the group does not validate or invalidate a group as a church. Jesus said, "Where two or three are gathered in my name, there am I in the midst of them." Our definition of the church has long been taken from that promise. A small church of twenty in one place considers itself very much a church, while in another place people do not feel they are a church. What makes the difference? Not size.

2. As you consider the reasons for your church's importance, do you need all the organization a larger congregation might have—or that your church may once have had? Remember that there is nothing sacred about the way you're organized. If you can no longer support a pastor as you once did, what other possibilities for spiritual leadership and ministry is God giving you? Is there someone in your own group who might be called forth by your fellowship, affirmed, and encouraged to seek some further training?

3. What are the possibilities for more fellowship with neighboring churches which may also be small?

4. Is there a possibility of sharing pastoral services with a sister congregation or a neighboring denomination? Do not consider merger too quickly.

5. What are the continuing needs, both local and world missionary needs? What new needs is God calling you to meet? This is a very important question and should have a bearing on all other questions you raise.

6. Is your church possibly being called into a new chapter of its life and mission by relocating in a nearby town or city rather than in its present rural location? Some congregations faced with this decision have made the move and today are vital growing churches. Others have chosen not to relocate and have continued to decline. This decision may need to be considered sooner than we think when we look carefully at how population trends in our area will affect our congregations.

7. If you are at the point where you feel led to disband, can you do so in a planned and purposeful way? By all means, plan

a big "homecoming" as a final celebration of the years God has led you together as a congregation, before you leave them behind as memories to follow His leading in another fellowship of His people.

8. Have you considered inviting someone to come in to help you assess your situation? It could be a wise step to take. Often looking at this kind of situation is so difficult for the people in the midst of it, because of deep feelings involved, that an outside facilitator is very much needed.

Churches are born. Churches grow. They mature. Some continue to gather and to minister in this world for many years. But churches also die. There is always some sadness when churches die, but sometimes we can make choices that open the possibility for life to continue in another setting—sometimes much like planting a new church. To see those choices and to make them with purposeful commitment often requires as much as or more courage than planting a new church.

DISCUSSION
1. Read 1 Corinthians 3:10. How do you understand what Paul means when he says, "I planted"?
2. Does everyone in your group know how your congregation got started? If not, find out. Tell the story. Write it.
3. As you read the guidelines for planting new churches, are there any about which you have questions? There are usually exceptions—can you cite examples? What were the important positive factors that were at work in the examples you have cited?
4. How might a new Mennonite church we plant be unique among the various kinds of new churches being planted today?

Notes
[1] *Church Growth Bulletin* (March 1977), p. 115.

encouraging growth

chapter 9

discovering our potential for growth

Church Growth Principle: *A growing congregation seeks to understand itself and analyzes the situation into which God has placed it.*

Attendance at worship and Sunday school at Wilmington Church of the Brethren is up by 40 percent since last year. Stewardship commitments have nearly doubled. There is a renewed sense of excitement about faith.

Allen T. Hansell, pastor of the congregation of 105 members, tells how it happened. "We were introduced to purposeful planning at a workshop which several of us attended in March. At our April board meeting we covenanted to discuss the process further in our May and June board meetings to make sure we understood it well. With that covenant we were on our way, not knowing at the time what a great experience we would have."

The members decided to use the Congregational Goals Discovery Plan developed by Commission on Home Ministries of the General Conference Mennonite Church. This plan suggests a step-by-step process which they used to set goals for 1978.

"Goal-setting is a long process," says Hansell, "and it does not work unless many people in the congregation commit themselves to it."

The pastor explained further that this process had done many things for them. First, it gave the members an opportunity to examine the total life of their congregation in a nonjudgmental way. Most members are aware only of "small pieces" of the church's life. They were pleasantly surprised to learn about things they didn't realize their church was doing. Secondly, the process made people feel that the church really does care and wants to know and meet their needs. Thirdly, the process fostered a high degree of goal ownership. Fourthly, the people got to know each other at deeper levels as they shared in the discovery groups. The question "What is God calling us to do?" became very real and personal. "We learned that the process is even more important than the goals that we shaped!" concluded pastor Hansell.

This third section of our study will suggest some ways a congregation can engage in planning that encourages growth. Purposeful planning is expectant planning. We do the hard work of planning with the anticipation of the new things God has promised to do!

Too often far-reaching decisions are made without taking the time to gather the facts and background information the Lord gives us to make the decisions. The Apostle Paul and his team planned ahead. We get glimpses of their planning in passages like Romans 15:18-33 where he shared his goal of going to Spain after delivering aid to the church at Jerusalem. Paul had assessed his ministry as complete where he had been (15:23), and Spain was largely untouched by the gospel.

There are various approaches to planning in the church. Where tradition is most important, planning will tend to be directed by the way things have been done in the past. Another approach can be called "the squeaking wheel gets the grease." This is a problem-oriented approach to planning. It is not really planning so much as it is reacting to problems. Whatever is most pressing now gets attention. Next month or next week it may be something else. This kind of "planning" lacks direction and purpose. It becomes discouraging because it focuses on problems rather than possibilities, and there are always enough new problems to keep us busy. Obviously, problems need to be faced and dealt with, but they cannot be allowed to direct our planning.

I would like to propose an approach to planning that is purposeful, goal-oriented, and more open to the creative leading of the Holy Spirit. This approach looks for *possibilities* rather than the problems. It focuses on our assets—the strengths, gifts, and resources God has given us—rather than on our liabilities. It encourages new ideas rather than only remedies to problems. It is future oriented rather than past oriented. It will encourage hopeful attitudes rather than pessimism. It encourages newcomers to participate because their ideas and contributions are also helpful in planning for the future.

Above all, our planning needs to grow out of expectant prayer and openness to the Holy Spirit's leading. The church at Antioch (Acts 11:29, 30; 13:1-3) was Spirit-led in its planning. It was while the people were worshiping the Lord and fasting that the Holy Spirit revealed a new strategy to them for getting the gospel out to their world. They were responsive to needs and innovative in sending the first missionaries. Purposeful planning that encourages us to look forward to new things to which God is calling us can help us become more mission oriented in our church.

What are the steps in purposeful planning? Usually there are five basic steps. First, we clarify our purpose. (See Chapter II for a discussion of clarification of purpose.) Second, we make an assessment of the present situation. Third, we determine our priorities. Fourth, we shape our goals. And fifth, we implement follow-through. Before we begin this cycle again we can evaluate the results and review our programs. Evaluation is part of assessment in the new planning cycle for an ongoing ministry.

In this chapter we shall discuss steps two, three, and four: assessment, prioritizing, and shaping goals. Follow-through planning will be discussed in Chapter 10.

Making an assessment. There is more than one way of making an assessment. Our reasons for doing the assessment will determine the way we do it, the kind of questions we ask, and the kind of information we gather to examine. For example, a growing church with increasingly crowded facilities might automatically assume they need a larger building. But it would be wiser to do a careful assessment of possibilities to help choose the best options for the future and help to decide about next steps that will encourage further growth. Or a congregation that has had frequent pastoral changes in the past ten years may wish to understand better why this has been happening and what their goals should be in light of that. They will likely do a different kind of assessment.

What are the occasions for a more thorough assessment? They vary. One congregation may come to an anniversary year and feel that an assessment and goal-setting process would be appropriate to their celebration of the anniversary. Another may see its surrounding neighborhood changing. Wanting to understand the changes better in order to plan accordingly, the congregation decides to make a careful assessment of its situation. Another congregation may feel it needs to revise its constitution. A careful overall assessment is important preparation for rewriting a constitution.

Once we have considered our reasons for wanting to do an assessment, it may be wise to seek some guidance from materials prepared for this. There are helpful tools available to do an assessment and set goals.[1]

The help of an outside person who can be more objective than we who are personally part of our situation is also helpful. This is like consulting a doctor for a health check-up. The doctor has training and experience in doing an assessment of our health. By asking us questions and administering certain tests the doctor not only tries to understand our condition better, but often helps us to be clearer about it ourselves. An outside person coming in to help with an assessment of our church and our neighborhood brings experience and objectivity and can ask the necessary questions. But while a doctor prescribes what we need to do, an outside congregational consultant should allow us to discern and to decide what God would have us do in the light of what our assessment process has helped us to see. The consultant might make suggestions and recommendations, but the responsibility for decision and action would be left to us.

Another principle for a congregation as a believer's church to remember in doing an assessment is that the Holy Spirit speaks through the whole congregation—not only through the leaders. Every member counts! Those who are affected by the decisions and involved in carrying out the follow-through plans should also be involved in the assessment and goal-setting. The pastor or the church board often have goals, but if these are not also the goals of the congregation, the chances of seeing them accomplished are diminished. There is no better way for the whole congregation to develop a sense of responsibility and enthusiasm for the ministries of the church than for them to be involved from the beginning in planning for these ministries.

What are some important questions to ask in making an assessment? One important question is *"What are our resources? Our strengths? Our gifts?"* To begin by raising our awareness of these—even doing an inventory of them—helps us to plan from strength rather than weakness.

One congregation, when it looked at itself, saw that it had a high percentage of older members. There were also many older persons in the neighborhood. The church members could have said, "What we lack is young couples," and made that the basis for their goal. That would have been planning from weakness because the weakest aspect of their congregational life and program was with young adults. The strongest area of community need was with older persons, not young adults. Instead, they saw that they had resources in the large percentage of older members. They set goals in these areas. They mobilized their people to meet the needs of older persons in the community. They organized and trained several older members for home visitation. Some new women's sewing and quilting groups were formed. A weekly noon lunch and social hour was started. Bible study groups were organized. The result was both spiritual and numerical growth.

Another important question is about our *identity. Who are we? How clear is who we are to our neighbors? Is this the way we want to be known? Does our identity reflect the Spirit of Christ as clearly as possible?* We need to find ways of hearing how others are seeing us. This is important because people outside of Christ and the church often do not hear the words of the gospel until they see it in "living letters" (1 Thess. 1:8, 9; 2 Cor. 3:2, 3). The question of who we are relates closely to the role of our church in our community. Is our church known for its Sunday school? Is it known for its music? Is it known for its ministry to alcoholics? Is it known for its strong involvement in peacemaking? Do we as leaders and members understand this and like the role we have? Or is our role in the community unclear? This is so important that it must be clarified before helpful goal-setting can take place.

A third area to assess is the *needs of our own members.* Carefully prepared surveys can be used. An every member visitation by teams of visitors is one way to assess member needs. It is also a systematic way of encouraging better communication within the congregation. Begin positively. Ask for something that was helpful; something people liked or appreciated; or something good that happened to them. Then also ask what they wish could have happened that did not. Ask for specific concerns. The result of such a visitation must also be shared with the whole congregation (in ways that do not betray confidences) in preparation for setting some new goals.

A fourth important area is the *needs of the world around us.* An assessment should help us to see the opportunities for service and witness in our nieghborhood, our city, and our world. Among other things, it should help us to see the potential for service and witness God has given us where we are and to plan for it. What are the needs of our immediate neighbors? Our town? The larger world community?

For our awareness of the needs of the larger world and ways of responding to them we work through our conference mission boards and relief organizations. But in our local community we can do more direct assessment ourselves. Who are the people in our community? How well do we know our neighbors and those with whom we work? What are their needs? These are some of the kinds of questions we can ask as we seek to understand our community.

What changes are occurring in the community? Has

population increased or declined? These facts can be obtained from the local government offices, chamber of commerce, public library, schools, or city planning offices to see what the trends seem to be.

Discerning responsiveness to the gospel. Discovering the possibilities for outreach in our community also means understanding who the responsive persons are and where they are. This does not mean neglecting all others, but it means that we want to be sure to share the gospel with those who have "ears to hear" it now.

What are some indicators of responsiveness? Persons who are new arrivals and who are without "roots"—friends, or established patterns in our community—will be more open to our sharing with them than persons who are longtime residents. Persons who are experiencing a major change in their lives such as marriage, the arrival of a baby, a serious illness, or a new job are often open to reconsidering a relationship to Christ and the church. Persons with whom we already have some things in common will be more open to our sharing the gospel with them than persons very different from ourselves.

It is clearly the purpose of God to reconcile all the differing peoples to Himself and to one another. Does the church work against that purpose by encouraging Spanish, Indian, black, or white congregations to develop rather than having all congregations integrated? Not necessarily. In recent decades there have been serious efforts to develop truly integrated congregations, but few of these grew. Does that mean we failed? Not necessarily. Some have grown. For reasons we have not always understood, however, people need their racial or cultural or ethnic identity as well as their sense of personal identity. We learned in foreign missions that to ignore this or to violate it thoughtlessly hindered rather than helped the long-range effectiveness of a missionary effort. Today we find ourselves, on the home front, learning some of those same lessons. While the integrated congregations toward which we once worked have not all grown, we are now seeing a new surge of rapid growth in our single culture groups, such as our

110

Menno-latino churches. This is the most rapidly growing segment of the Mennonite church in North America.

Nor does the failure of most integrated congregations to grow mean that the gospel has failed. It may mean rather that we have too seldom understood how such churches develop. And God may also use other ways to accomplish His purpose of a "church universal." God has, for example, used certain cross-cultural persons to move from one cultural group to another just as He used Philip, a Hellenist, in Acts 8 to move beyond the Jews to the Samaritans. He used Paul, a non-Palestinian Jew who had grown up in Gentile Tarsus, to move beyond the Jewish church to Gentiles of his world.

While individual congregations may not be integrated, the oneness of the whole body can also be celebrated in inter-congregational and inter-conference fellowship. Thus a denomination like the Mennonites can celebrate the oneness of the church across cultural and racial lines in conference gatherings such as the 1978 World Conference in Wichita with its many kinds of people represented. The important question is not simply if we have people of different colors in our congregations, but whether or not we can truly welcome them into our lives. There must be a complete welcome to anyone who would come to Christ. That already makes them our brothers and sisters in Christ. "Welcome one another . . . as Christ has welcomed you" (Rom. 15:7). That means making them part of our congregation. Segregation is sin because it tries to keep people out, whether it is because they are nonwhite, non-American, non-Mennonite, or whatever the reason. Encouraging congregations to reach those in their own culture does not mean promoting the attitude of segregation!

But what do we do if there aren't very many people of our culture around us? If our congregations represent a subculture so different from all the people around us, much of our evangelism will be cross-cultural. If we are resistant to becoming more open to persons of other backgrounds, we need at least to encourage and support those persons from our midst who are more "cross-cultural" in their attitudes to establish new fellowships alongside our established congregations for now, and trust the Lord to make us one in spirit and in truth, even though culturally different. Perhaps in ten years or thirty years from now, there will have been a growing understanding and acceptance of one another's culture as well.

Spirit-directed common sense is important in an assessment process. It is possible to get bogged down in endless detailed analysis, unless only helpful information is selected and included in the analysis. Nor is a thorough-going overall assessment necessary every year. Once a more creative step-by-step planning approach is learned it can be applied in whatever ways are most appropriate and helpful each year. Each organization within the congregation can also learn to plan creatively—seeking information to basic questions like the ones suggested above, but adapted to its organization and purpose. "Seek ye first the kingdom of God and his righteousness" is Jesus' clear reminder that some things must be put ahead of others in our lives. What is most important even within kingdom work? What needs attention now? None of us can do everything. No congregation can carry out all the ministries that are needed. Prioritizing is especially important for smaller congregations, because they cannot and need not have all the organizational structures or programs that larger congregations have.

Prioritizing can be done by taking what we have learned in the assessment and asking, "What is our greatest strength and our best resource? What are the most pressing needs? How would our resources fit those needs?" For example, in one growing church in Ohio it became apparent that the most pressing need was for more pastoral caring relationships for the new people, many of whom were new Christians. The pastor was no longer able to carry out his pastoring functions as adequately as before. At the same time, the church members realized that the Lord had also given them the resources of several persons in the congregation with Christian maturity and pastoral gifts. It became, at this point in their congregational life, a high priority aspect to which they decided to give prayerful attention during the next year.

But if our church has not been growing even though located

in the midst of potential for growth, faithfulness to the Lord may mean giving the things that make for growth new priority. Outreach itself may need to be given a new priority. For a maintenance-oriented congregation to begin to become a truly mission-oriented congregation is often like getting a rocket off the ground. Huge engines and immense amounts of fuel are needed. But once it's in orbit these engines drop off and much smaller engines are sufficient. A major commitment of time, energy, and resources may be needed for several years. A heavy program of maintenance-oriented activities may need to be thoroughly reviewed and revised to free the people who are now so busy with "church work" that they don't have time or energy for mission-oriented work of the church.

Setting goals in new priority areas can help us to get reoriented. But it will not be quick or easy. Be prepared for much prayer, perseverance, and patience.

Setting faith goals. The next step in planning is to shape goals in those areas that are to be given priority attention. What is a goal? A goal is different from a statement of purpose. A goal states *what* we believe the Holy Spirit is directing us to accomplish. A statement of purpose is a general statement of why we exist, what our overall aim is, and *why* we do what we do. The Ohio congregation referred to above knows that part of the purpose of its church is to be a caring community of faith. As a goal for the next year it feels led to emphasize, "We want to become a more caring church so that every person may be helped to grow." Such a goal statement, however, is refined even further by shaping specific objectives. For example, one objective might be "to have discovered by the end of this year an acceptable way to strengthen our pastoral care ministry." Goal statements are more focused than our overall purpose. Objectives are even more specific, datable, and measurable than goal statements. Often there are several objectives contributing to the same goal.

One rural congregation discovered that about one-third of the people in the area did not attend church anywhere on Sunday morning. It had not expected the percentage to be so high, so it made a new commitment to its missionary purpose.

It set a new goal "to strengthen our outreach to the unchurched in our area in the next year." One of the measurable objectives was "to visit with twenty-five unchurched families in our area during the next twelve months." A second objective was "to hold at least four events in the church in the next year designed for the larger community."

To ask, "What are the goals for our church?" is another way of asking, "What is the Lord's will for our church?" Nehemiah gives us a clear biblical illustration of how a vision (rebuilding Jerusalem) is followed by careful assessment, goal-setting, and follow-through. He surveyed the ruins of Jerusalem, set goals for rebuilding, and proceeded to organize the work force around specific parts of the task to get the job done (Neh. 1:1—6:15).

A goal is a statement of faith. Goals should challenge us. Clear goals and specific objectives can help a group work together. They help us to make our Christian commitment real. Clear goals and measurable objectives help to focus our follow-through planning. To set even a few clear goals can make us more conscious of the fact that we usually have goals and objectives in what we do, though we have not often articulated them clearly.

DISCUSSION

1. Do you have questions about the five-phase purposeful planning process suggested in this chapter?
2. Review the story of Nehemiah in Nehemiah 1:1—6:15. Identify the various steps he followed in planning.
3. At what times in the life of the congregation would such thoughtful planning be especially helpful?
4. Does this approach to planning suggest some changes for the way we conduct our annual congregational meetings?

Notes
[1]One such tool is the *Congregational Goals Discovery Plan* published by the Commission on Home Ministries of the General Conference Mennonite Church.

chapter 10

planning expectantly

Church Growth Principle: *A growing congregation plans expectantly.*

Lincoln Glen Mennonite Brethren Church, a congregation located in a highly mobile suburban community, was getting discouraged about its outreach. With the help of the new pastor it investigated and learned the key reasons why results were so limited.

On the basis of what they had learned the members decided to develop a whole new plan for outreach—a friendship evangelism program that would involve four phases: (1) Prayer support—all would be encouraged to be part of a prayer chain system; (2) Friendship—as new families visit the Sunday service or are discovered in the community, a volunteer family from the church whose interests matched those of the new family would be asked to offer friendship to the new family. They would have one month to arrange and carry out a social engagement with the new family. If the friendship "clicked" they would build it further. They would be the ones to introduce them to their Sunday school and/or other groups in the church; (3) Visitation—a smaller number who would work directly with the pastor would visit in new homes as visitation teams from the church; and (4) Assimilation—into "watch care families." As new persons or families would come to know Christ or reaffirm their faith and come into the congregation, they would be assigned to one of the watch care families under the leadership of a deacon couple who would shepherd them through preparation for membership and continue to be available for pastoral care.

The new plan was implemented by inviting each member to personalize his or her commitment to outreach by volunteering for some specific part of the plan.

It was not easy. It took much patience and encouragement. Workshops were held on prayer, on how to offer friendship, on sharing the gospel naturally, and other needed topics. The plan began to work. This congregation has grown from 394 to 500 since 1974. New faces appear more often. They have seen God changing lives, both of new persons and of long-term members!

Have you ever visited somewhere and come away saying to yourself, "They certainly have a tremendous evangelism program! And they have a fantastic musical program. If only we had programs like that, things would be different in our church"?

Churches with well-run programs seem to grow because of their programs, but a program is not the first thing we need. Factors like the positive hopeful attitudes of members, qualities of real love and joy in our fellowship, strong Bible teaching, and good leadership are all more basic to the growth of the church than a certain right program. Yet it must be said that solid continuing commitment to Jesus as Lord and seeking to meet human need helpfully in the name of Christ require that things be done in an orderly manner. This leads to well-planned and well-run programs.

Spiritual renewal may bring new commitment and enthusiasm for Christ, but left completely to spontaneous further expression, it lacks direction and discipline. Leaders with the gift of administration are needed. Orderly programs can help us channel new joy and commitment to Christ to make it more helpful to others and fruitful in the kingdom.

In this chapter we want to examine how a church can follow assessment, prioritizing, and goal-setting with the kind of program planning and implementation that further encourages growth. The point of this chapter is to help congregations do more program planning of their own. One of the marks of a growing church is creative adaptation and/or development of the kinds of programs that are right for its situation.

Once goals and objectives have been clearly discerned, we are ready to ask, "How would God have us work toward them? How are present programs working toward them? What new plans will we need?" We can be confident that the Holy Spirit will further stir our imagination and give us eyes to see what needs to be done. But by all means, get started. Don't wait for the "super-idea." Begin with the ideas you have—however ordinary they seem. Accept them as the Spirit's gifts to you. Accept them as having possibilities.

The Evangelism Committee at First Church had been asked to do the follow-through planning toward the congregational goal of sharing the gospel with new persons in a meaningful way during the next year. One of the objectives was "to learn to know twenty-five new persons well enough to share the gospel with them." This was the first time these people had had a goal like this. They had not been a growing church. They began with a time of prayer. Then chairman Bill suggested that all six of them gather around the table.

"Let's begin by thinking of all the possible ways we could do this," he suggested. "I'll give you each several pieces of blank paper on which you can write your idea after you share it with the committee. Let's start with you, Sue, and go on around the table."

"We could plan to visit twenty-five homes," she offered.

"Write that down on one of your papers," Bill replied.

"I think we'd do better to plan a special musical night at church and invite the whole neighborhood," Joe volunteered. "That way we'd see who was interested in our church."

"Write that on a piece of paper," Bill instructed.

Now it was Rosella's turn. "I believe we'd need to get to know the people personally first in order for the sharing to be meaningful," she said.

"OK, write 'Get to know new people personally' on your paper, Rosie," suggested Bill. "Some more ideas, please. Keep them coming!"

Jim hesitated, but then offered, "Well, I don't know about the rest of you, but I feel the need for more training in sharing my faith meaningfully. I'll be honest—I don't make a practice of talking to people much about my faith. I just don't feel like I know how."

"Thanks, Jim. Be sure to put that suggestion on a piece of paper. Would you say, 'Training for sharing our faith'?"

Ralph was the youngest member of the committee. "I really wonder how welcome new people would be in our church if they decided to come here. I think we might have to train the whole congregation to accept new people more readily."

"Is that an idea for something we might do that you can write down in a few words? Write it down, Ralph."

Ralph wrote in large letters, "TRAIN WHOLE CONGRE-GATION TO BE MORE FRIENDLY."

The committee went on gathering ideas until no one could think of any more. "Great! Let's collect these ideas and look at all of them again. If we think of things we're already doing as a church, let's see where that might fit in. I'll write our goal and our objective at the far right end of this long plain white sheet of planning paper and then let's decide which of these ideas we want to choose as possible steps toward it."

As they looked over all the ideas they had suggested, certain ones began to emerge as most appealing and appropriate. They placed several on the planning sheet and talked about the sequence in which they would need to happen. They penciled in target dates.

"Now, let's look at what we need to be doing before our next committee meeting next month."

One by one they accepted responsibility for various things that needed to be done as their names were penciled onto the planning sheet with a brief note. Chairman Bill realized that knowing exactly what they need to do helps committee members to get their part of the job done. He also felt free to delegate responsibilities appropriately.

They closed with prayer that included specific matters they now knew they were going to be responsible for. The planning sheet was rolled up and laid on the shelf in the church office

118

where anyone who needed to see it could find it. If they'd had room, they might have put it up on the wall where it could remain posted.

At the next church board meeting, Bill reported on the initial planning that the Evangelism Committee had done. It gave the board a chance to ask questions and comment.

When the committee met at its next monthly meeting, each one reported in. It became clear now that some of their planning would have to be changed. But other things were confirmed. Ralph's earlier suggestion to "train the whole congregation for friendliness and acceptance" was reshaped into concrete ways members could offer not only "friendliness" but also "friendship" to new persons. A Hospitality Plan was developed whereby members could volunteer to be prepared on a given Sunday to invite guests for Sunday dinner. Volunteers were scheduled so that every Sunday was covered. And when there were no visitors to invite, they invited someone else from the congregation they hadn't yet gotten to know very well. The committee asked people who could to pledge themselves to offer friendship to one new person or couple during the coming year, and offered a seminar on "How to Make Friends."

Jim's original suggestion for training in sharing our faith was taking shape in plans for a twelve-week series in which the pastor and a person from the congregation who had some experience in personal evangelism teamed up to lead a small group in some classroom and "on-the-job" training in witnessing.

Unlike evangelism committees who don't know what to do, the Evangelism Committee of First Church had a goal to give their planning some direction and focus. Not everything the committee thought of doing worked out. There were some disappointments. The Evangelism Committee members had to spend more time than they expected encouraging one another and certain members who volunteered at first but got discouraged. Yet as they checked their records by the end of the first year, they could identify twenty new persons with whom someone from their congregation had had the opportunity to share the gospel meaningfully. It was also the first year in a long time that they had had adult baptisms—three of them! Seven other adults joined by transfer. In each case, when you asked the new members why they joined First Church, they said, "We found friends here." And First Church itself began to change!

Suggestions to remember for follow-through planning. What are some important principles of follow-through planning? First, be sure you understand your goal and objectives clearly. Make sure they are stated in terms of end results you believe, by faith, can be accomplished. For example, someone at first suggested that the evangelism goal for First Church be: "To add twenty-five new people to our congregation by the end of next year." There are several difficulties with a goal like that. It does not say what we mean by "adding new people." Does that mean new members, or is regular attendance enough? Does it mean a net increase of twenty-five by the end of the year? It further does not allow sufficiently for the fact that we cannot compel people to trust Christ or to join. This is a large factor beyond our ability to accomplish. We trust the Lord to bring them to repentance and faith, and to commitment to the church body. God gives the growth. It is better for us to shape our goals and objectives to include the things for which we can also accept as much responsibility as possible.

When a need is identified and a goal is set, it is wise to find out what is already being done to meet that need. For example, if your goal is one designed to meet the needs of a growing number of teenage girls bearing children out of wedlock in your area, find out what the other concerned groups in the community, such as schools, public welfare, and adoption services, are doing about the need. The congregation would be well advised to learn all it can from those agencies about what they are doing before it makes plans for a ministry to address that need.

A third principle of follow-through is to get an overall strategy in mind before getting too detailed on any point. Effective leaders know this almost intuitively. Adjustments can always be made, but this will keep us from getting as easily sidetracked in our follow-through planning. It also helps the group to see the relatedness of what each is doing with the other's part of the task.

Fourth, as chairperson, respond positively to the suggestions of your committee. If an idea is not a usable one, let the committee discern that together rather than becoming the sole judge of whether a suggestion is usable or impractical.

Fifth, be clear in assignments to individuals. Delegate tasks and expect people to get them done. Trust them to do them. When you've asked someone to do something, do not fail to call for a report from that person. This builds confidence and accountability.

Sixth, remember to express your appreciation to one another. Even in the planning, a word of appreciation is often in order. Genuine affirmation of one another is one of the ways we show love for one another.

Seventh, help the whole congregation to personalize the goal. In order for group goals to be achieved, many persons need to do their part. They are often willing, but do not know just what that part is unless our plans clearly suggest how.

Eighth, communicate. We have not communicated until we are understood as well as heard. More planning breaks down because of inadequate communication than any other factor. Especially when introducing a new idea or plan in the congregation as a whole, we can not assume it has been heard with one explanation. Most people need to "hear" it at least three times, preferably in three different ways, before it is understood.

If yours is the kind of goal that needs to be kept before the whole congregation, do that with regular references to it. With some kinds of goals, the numbers related to it are primarily important for the committee and the church board to keep as measurement. The sharing in the congregation in such cases is best done in terms of what is happening rather than in terms of numbers. The numerical aspect of any goal is, after all, not as important as what God is doing in people's lives and relationships. We share and celebrate what God is doing!

121

But keep some records of what you do. Keeping records is part of good pastoral care, good stewardship, and good administration of plans. We have learned the importance of careful record-keeping of money. Can we be equally diligent about "people-records"?

Records should not be kept only for the sake of records. We keep attendance records, for example, not only for assessment and goal setting, but also to help us be more aware of the needs of people. Changes in a person's attendance and participation are often a signal. In the larger group activities, such as corporate worship, a change in attendance patterns by individuals can tell the leaders that something may have happened in that person's life of which we need to become aware. Studies have shown that many persons in the church, when they experience a crisis in their lives, do not actively seek the counsel and support they need from the church. They begin to withdraw instead of reaching out to others openly for help. However, an alert pastor or leader will recognize such signals of need and respond to them. It has been found that the first three to six weeks of a person's withdrawal are a crucial time for the church fellowship to seek to respond in caring ways. Many, although not all, who have become inactive have been allowed to do so through a difficult experience in which they needed special care which they not only found hard to accept, but were also not offered by church leaders or members who were unresponsive at the time of need.

In summary, planning expectantly grows out of our vision of God's purpose for us. It is nourished by prayer, directed by the Holy Spirit, and led by committed persons using the spiritual gift of administration. It means being willing to learn the disciplines of purposeful planning so that the ministries of the church can be more effective and we may be found faithful in our stewardship of the resources God has given us for the purpose to which He calls us.

DISCUSSION

1. Look up and share the following references to planning from Proverbs: 13:16; 14:8; 18:13; 15:22; 16:1; 13:19; 18:15. Read each

from a KJV, RSV, ASV, or NIV first and then from *The Living Bible*.

2. How would you respond to the person who suggests that we should give less attention to planning and simply follow the Spirit more?

3. What do you think makes planning such hard work for some of us?

chapter 11

gifts for growth

Church Growth Principle: *A growing church uses the many gifts of the Spirit for worship, fellowship, and outreach.*

The Mennonite Church at Springfield, Ohio, had grown from thirty-five to nearly 200 in three years. It began to realize that more persons were needed to serve alongside the pastor in pastoral care for members and families. The members spent one month studying the scriptural qualities of an elder, and the gifts that an elder might have for ministry. Then they asked each person to take one week to pray and to decide who in the congregation had the spiritual maturity and gifts to serve as an elder. "Think of the one person you'd most likely go to with a need or problem if the pastor were not available," they were instructed. When they gathered the following week, each one was to write one name on a slip of paper.

Out of that process, five persons were named most often. Each was asked whether he also felt the Lord was calling him to serve, and whether he could work alongside the present pastor. In this way a group of elders was chosen and affirmed by the whole congregation. No election was held. It was agreed that three years hence they would review how things had worked out and decide how to continue. Their continuing growth as a congregation was further encouraged.

Understanding gifts. The church is a body. That means it is a living organism, not simply an organization. As we live out

124

God's purpose for us, as we work toward faith goals, and as we seek to accomplish our objectives, the Holy Spirit gives us the abilities we need. John Driver, in his book *Community and Commitment,* calls the church "a community of gifts."

What do we mean by gifts? In a broad sense, gifts may include such things as natural talent, material wealth, and qualities of character. Talents are actually gifts. We can develop them, but we do not earn them. Material things, though we think we've earned them, are also only entrusted to us for stewardship. Qualities of character are partially the gifts to us of our parents and family. Believers and unbelievers all share in this kind of "giftedness." In a broad sense, gifts can be thought of as all those things that help to make us the unique person each of us is.

Using the term "gifts" to refer to "spiritual gifts" sometimes excludes such things as natural talent, material possessions, and qualities of character, in order to focus on those abilities which are empowered by the Holy Spirit in the believer (Rom. 5:5). New Testament passages such as 1 Corinthians 12, Romans 12:3-8, Ephesians 4:7-13, and 1 Peter 4:10, 11 are some key references to the spiritual gifts. In this definition, gifts of the Spirit are not the same as fruit of the Spirit (Gal. 5:22, 23). Spiritual gifts vary from person to person, whereas the fruit of the Spirit can be expected as evidence of the Holy Spirit's presence in every Christian's life. Thus "love" is a basic fruit of the Spirit rather than a spiritual gift. By comparison, the fruits of the Spirit are emphasized far more in the New Testament than are the gifts of the Spirit. This may suggest where our greatest emphasis also needs to be.

Faith is a gift of the Spirit, but it is spoken of in more than one way. Saving faith is to trust in Christ for salvation (Eph. 2:8, 9) and to obey Him as Lord. The gift of faith (1 Cor. 12:9) is the ability to see and work toward possibilities which others cannot yet see.

Several further observations should be kept in mind from a study of spiritual gifts in the Scriptures. First, the Holy Spirit is the giver of these gifts and gives them as He chooses, not as we may choose. The Greek word for gifts, *charismata,* suggests that they are the gifts of grace, *charis* (Rom. 12:6). Thus, they are gifts in the life of the believer and in the life of the believing fellowship that acknowledges the grace of God. Second, the gifts are given to the whole body, not only to certain individuals (1 Cor. 12:12-26; Rom. 12:3-5) in the body. Third, the gifts are given to glorify Christ (1 Cor. 12:1-4). That is, they are not given for self-enhancement but for the good of the whole body in worship, fellowship, and service to others. Fourth, the gifts are always to be exercised in love (1 Cor. 13). Without love, they can quickly become an empty egotistical exercise.

There is nothing to indicate that any of the gifts are limited to the apostolic age. This means they may all be manifested in our day as in the days of the apostles. And just as in their day, there are false expressions of the spiritual gifts which are not of the Holy Spirit. The gift of discernment is needed in our day, as then, to "test the spirits" (1 John 4:1), to sense whether the gifts are being expressed out of love, and to know whether they stand the test Jesus gives us: "You will know them by their fruits" (Matt. 7:20).

The lists which appear in 1 Corinthians 12 and Romans 12 do not appear to be exhaustive. Hence, as we discern the working of the Spirit in our day, we may name yet other gifts which meet the above definition and qualifications as valid gifts of the Spirit.

Gifts for mission. In this chapter we want to examine the relationship between gifts and the growth of the church. One of the functions of the church is to help members discover, develop, and employ the gifts that God has given them even in the broad definition of that term as given above. We have sometimes perceived gift discernment as a better way to select people for the various church offices. While our selection of persons for special responsibilities and roles should include discernment of their gifts, it should involve careful consideration of other qualifications for leadership as well (1 Tim. 3; Titus 1:5-9). Gift discernment in the local congregation is not synonymous with the usual function of a nominating committee.

126

Discerning and affirming gifts helps everyone to discover and to exercise ministry (1 Pet. 4:10, 11). The College Church, Northampton, Massachusetts, asks all new members for a two-fold commitment: to Christ and to a ministry in the community. Persons are helped to identify their ministry through a process of counseling and gift discernment as they become members. The church also helps each one with a "placement." While the church has been growing steadily, its numerical growth is really a by-product. The first commitment is to Christ and to ministering to the community as a servant church.[1]

Gift discernment in a broad sense is an authentic dimension of being the church. In Romans 12:3-6, Paul emphasizes that each believer should think of himself with "sober judgment," realistically, not too highly nor too lowly. Galatians 6:3 also emphasizes that one of the marks of a Spirit-filled fellowship is an honest estimate of oneself and one's abilities. It soon becomes apparent that gift discernment helps each believer to a clearer sense of who he or she is as a new person in Christ (2 Cor. 5:17). Coming to a clearer sense of self-identity in this way is essential to a deeper realization of the meaning of salvation itself in our lives. This means that gift discernment in the Christian fellowship has an important bearing on many aspects of our lives, such as our vocational choices, our decision about marriage, and our pursuit of further education, as well as the way we participate in the life of the congregation and the direct ministries of the church.[2]

Why gift discernment facilitates growth. Congregations where gift discernment is happening will grow because they are meeting a spiritual need we all have, namely, to learn to know better who we are in Christ. Members of such churches will give up promotions, even jobs, rather than move away from a Christian fellowship where they are experiencing that! As the gifts are affirmed and used, the spiritual health of a local congregation is enhanced. A healthy fellowship grows.

Affirmation of the spiritual gifts also brings a more creative, alive, and spontaneous worship life to the local congregation. As we have noted in Chapter IV, congregations with a vital

127

experience of corporate worship tend to be growing congregations.

Affirming the gifts also encourages growth as it strengthens the outreach ministries specifically. There are those in every congregation, for example, with the gift of evangelism. They need our affirmation and encouragement even as those with the gift of teaching or singing. While all believers are witnesses (Acts 1:8), there are some who are gifted to be evangelists (Eph. 4:11, 12).

The gift of evangelism does not necessarily mean having "the gift of gab." God chooses people with various kinds of personality for this gift. Some elements that persons with the gift of evangelism have in common are: (1) an experiential knowledge of the gospel, with a quiet inner certainty about their own salvation; (2) a particular sensitivity to where other persons are in their life experience which helps them sense when they are ready to make a personal commitment to Jesus Christ; (3) the knack for getting close to persons to help them to make a personal commitment to Christ; (4) and the ability to share the gospel clearly and appropriately in the situation where they are. Persons with the gift of evangelism enjoy these "close encounters" and see opportunities to share the gospel which many of us might not see. They are self-starters in witnessing. They see positive results from their witnessing.

To recognize the gift of evangelism in certain people, however, does not mean that the evangelists are the only ones who do evangelism. Evangelism is still the task of the whole congregation. It is also still part of the pastor's task, even though it may not be his clearest gift. Paul instructs Timothy to "do the work of an evangelist" (2 Tim. 4:5). There are ways in which we participate in the work of evangelism, whether we have the gift or not. Our attitude and the climate of the whole fellowship have a decisive bearing on whether the gift of evangelism will be exercised.

Gift discernment encourages growth because it helps believers to know more clearly what gifts they do *not* have. It is a mistake to assume that every member of the body should take a turn in every responsibility in the group for the sake of equal sharing. This assumption is like expecting the ear to function as a hand (1 Cor. 12) without recognizing that they are quite differently equipped as different parts of the body. To know more clearly what gifts we do not have, therefore, can be relieving. It can help us to say "No" when we need to say "No," not simply out of modesty or feelings of inadequacy. However, this is not to suggest that we become so narrowly specialized or so rigid in our attitudes that we will never try some new activity.

Actually, most of us have not only one gift, but a cluster of gifts—some of which may currently be stronger than others. The Spirit may also choose to bless us with new gifts at some point. But seldom, if ever, is even one member given all the gifts so that "taking turns" in all the functions of the body makes sense. Knowing which gifts we do not have, as well as knowing which gifts we have, makes for a freer and more joyful participation by members in the life of the congregation.

Some practical suggestions. The process of discerning and affirming spiritual gifts in local congregations varies considerably. It is really a part of the ongoing life of the congregation.

Congregations in which there has been conflict over the gifts of the Spirit face special problems which may make it difficult to be helpful to one another in gift discernment. Sometimes the hesitation grows out of a special apprehension about certain spiritual gifts, such as tongues or healing, which have been overemphasized. A period of patient teaching on the Holy Spirit and spiritual gifts in the church may be helpful as preparation.

Congregations which are not accustomed to interacting on a personal level may also find it embarrassing to focus on gift discernment because gift discernment can become very personal. Often, once some of the embarrassment has been overcome, the experience of having a group help us identify more clearly what strengths and gifts they see in us becomes in itself a very affirming experience. Attending a special introductory workshop can be helpful. Visiting other congregations where they do seek to discern the gifts of members can also be helpful. We can ask questions and learn from them.

Few tools for gift discernment are available, though more are being designed and tried. Using them can be helpful, but they should be seen as giving us helpful clues rather than conclusive answers.[3]

The process of gift discernment involves both personal reflection and group interaction. One without the other is never as helpful as some combination of both.

Personal reflection can begin as we ask ourselves what kinds of things we have done quite well. What have I enjoyed doing? Have I been willing to try a variety of ways of serving to experiment with as many possibilities as I can? What have been the results? What have others asked me to do? Why did they ask me?

Individual discernment is limited, however, because of our tendency to see ourselves from only one point of view—our own. We need the perspective of others and interaction with others to see our gifts more clearly.

Gifts discernment in a group. A group experience in gifts discernment happens best where members of the group have learned to know and trust one another. At some point in the group's life together they may wish to do a beginning exercise in gift discernment as follows (If the group is larger than six or eight, form smaller groups of four to six persons each.): (1) Let each one first, in a few minutes of silence, write on a slip of paper the strengths, abilities, or gifts they see in each of the other persons in the group. Then take a few more minutes for each one to write down his or her own gifts. (2) Beginning with the leader, let each one in the group be in the "spotlight" where the whole group focuses their attention. (3) Now let members of the group name what they have written for the one in the "spotlight." (4) Before moving the "spotlight" to the next person, let the person now in the "spotlight" also tell how he or she felt about what was named. It is important that gifts which others see in us also be confirmed in our own hearts. (5) After a time of praise and prayer, the members of the group may agree to take the coming week to reflect on one or more of the gifts the group has identified. (6) The following week they should report on what, if anything further, they feel they have learned during the week. There should be opportunity to raise further questions with the group about one's own gifts.

Another approach to group discernment of spiritual gifts may be around a particular project or task or mission. The Church of the Savior in Washington, D.C., for example, encourages each member to listen for a call to mission.[4] A mission or task may be any one of a variety of things like housing repair, tutoring schoolchildren who need help, prison ministries, or Christian education for children. If someone hears such a call, it is shared so others may also respond if they can hear that as a call. Then, the new group meets as a new mission group to consider how to carry out their calling. They take some time to learn to know one another and identify the gifts each one brings to the group. Persons in the group are named to the various roles and responsibilities as needed for the mission of the group according to their gifts. Thus discerning the gifts for serving follows the call to serve. They trust God not only to call, but to equip with the necessary gifts.

A helpful way to learn to do gift discernment together is to role play a call to mission. A role play can provide a nonthreatening situation in which we can discover some things about ourselves and each other that can be helpful later. You can role play a call to mission in your group by thinking of some need you would like to see met if you had the chance to do it. If your group is larger than ten persons you could have several persons share their "call." Have everyone in the group choose the "call" that interests them most. Try to have no more than ten and no less than five in any group. This may mean that some "calls" will not be used for this role play. Then in each group, ask what gifts each person has. Hear from the group and also from the individual. What roles will you need to carry out your mission?

In some congregations, nominating committees are being replaced by a standing gift discernment committee whose task it is to learn to know the gifts of everyone in the congregation. When someone is needed for a new task, this committee is consulted for help in recommending the right person to call to the new task. Gifts discernment, if taken seriously, can affect the way a congregation selects its leaders. Instead of holding an election in which there are winners and losers, the congregation enters into a time of study of Scripture regarding the qualifications, a time of prayer for guidance, and discernment of who has the spiritual maturity and gifts that are needed. While a gift discernment committee can help to select members for various responsibilities, the most important function of such a committee may well be to help each person in self-understanding and personal gifts discernment. Such a committee might consider how to give some guidance for gift discernment in the whole congregation.

To have a gift puts us under a call to use it. Not to use it is to treat it like the unfaithful servant in the parable of the talents who buried his talent rather than putting it to use for the Master (Matt. 25:14-30). Let us rather use the gifts God gives us for His service and for His glory.

DISCUSSION

1. Read the following passages: Romans 12:3-8; 1 Corinthians 12; 1 Peter 4:8-10; Ephesians 4:1-16. How would you define "gifts" as used in the four passages?
2. List the gifts which are named in some way in the passages listed above. Are there some you do not understand? Which of these gifts might be especially important for outreach?
3. Review Jesus' teachings regarding the Holy Spirit. What does He emphasize in passages like Luke 11:5-13; John 14:15-26; 15:26, 27; and 16:7-15?
4. What do you see as some reasons for increased interest recently in spiritual gifts in the church?
5. What comments or questions about the gifts of the Spirit does this chapter raise for you?

Notes
[1] Dan Bauman, *All Originality Makes a Dull Church* (Santa Ana, Calif.: Vision House, 1976), pp. 85-91.
[2] James Fairfield, *All That We Are We Give* (Scottdale: Herald Press, 1978), is an excellent study for a group seeking to learn more about gift discernment as part of our stewardship.
[3] See "Your Gifts and the Church" in the Leader's Guide to this book. A

132

more thorough self-assessment tool called *You and Your Options* by Palmer Becker is available from Box 347, Newton, KS 67114.

[4]A full description of the process the Church of the Savior uses can be found in Gordon Cosby's *Handbook for Mission Groups* (Waco, Texas: Word, Inc., 1975).

chapter 12

training for growth

Church Growth Principle: *A growing church trains its members for the tasks to which they are called.*

"Come along with me tonight," said Pastor Adam Esbenshade, "and you will meet some of the members of the church. We're having a Sunday school teacher training meeting."

"Humph," I thought. "All the way to New Haven, Connecticut, and just a Sunday school meeting. I wish I could see the *church*."

The Mennonite Bible Fellowship Church of New Haven is an inner-city fellowship—young, black, and growing. More and more, whole families are crowding into the little sanctuary, many of them now Christians.

That evening I witnessed a Sunday school teachers' meeting which blew my stereotypes. I watched while Pastor Adam set up a Sunday school class, and proceeded to demonstrate how to teach it. It was creative, practical, stimulating.

Afterward, he had a long conversation with one of the members, a young Christian. (Almost none of the members have been Christians longer than four years.) He asked Adam question after question: "How would you do this? How would you teach that?"

"New Christians soon take leadership here at New Haven," said Adam. "You *can* ask young believers to get involved too soon, but in most churches we err in the other direction. I just invite young

Christians to begin taking the same responsibilities they see other brothers and sisters taking, as they feel ready. This is *their* church—not the pastor's."

Why is training important? As I've been writing these chapters I've also been teaching this unit in a class of adults from week to week. Last week one of the men in the class said, "You have a lot of good theory here. What we need when we get through with this series is for you to help us put it into practice."

I was excited about his comment. He was expressing a desire not only to learn about how churches grow but also to participate in practical ways. When I asked the class what they felt would be most helpful to them, several said, "What I need most is some practical training in evangelism."

In this chapter we shall examine the nature of training. We shall use training for evangelism as an example although many of the same principles for effective training could be applied to other aspects of the mission of the church.

The request for practical training is one we need to hear because many conscientious church members want to serve well, but don't feel they know how to do it.

Why has practical training been neglected? When a congregation has lost the vision of being an enabling fellowship, there will not likely be practical training. When there is no vision of the church's mission, there will not likely be training for it.

Sometimes there has been no training for evangelism, for example, because it is assumed no training is needed—it is something Christians are to do spontaneously under the prompting of the Spirit. As described in Acts, in the early church "lay people" shared the gospel where they went (Acts 8:4). But in today's church it is estimated that very few of us share our faith in a way that helps another person make a personal commitment to Jesus Christ.

Training in evangelism is also neglected when we assume that all we need to do is exhort one another to do it! Sometimes pastors are very diligent to exhort members to witness in the hope of building a more evangelistic congregation. But if all we do is exhort one another, we may simply be adding to an already nagging sense of guilt that comes from good intentions never carried out. Exhortation is not the same as enabling. "Teach us how to do evangelism" may be the honest confession of persons who already feel guilty over their sense of failure. They have said "Yes" in their hearts and have a desire to share their faith. What they need is training that enables.

For second- and third-generation Christians, sharing their faith is often more difficult than for new Christians. It is not that they are not truly Christian. But their faith has become part of the very fabric of their lives, and they have not learned to make it explicit so they can tell someone else. We owe them more than exhortation.

The request "Teach us how" is one Jesus would honor. He devoted Himself to the training of the twelve for three years as He carried on His earthly ministry. He modeled ministry. At times He also gave explicit direct training. When, for example, He sent out the seventy (Luke 10:1ff) they were given specific instructions. When they returned He listened to their reports and used their experiences to teach them.

We need to honor the request for teaching not only because it is reasonable but also because it has great potential. Consider the results for the outreach of your congregation if members in your church were being helpfully trained to share their faith wherever they were in their world of personal contacts with relatives, at work, in school, at play, and in business. The early church grew because the gospel was shared along the network of the households and personal contacts new Christians already had.

Train new believers. Growing churches today have found that training their newest believers is very important, especially to strengthening their evangelistic outreach. Christians grow in their new relationships to Christ as they share it. New Christians have the largest number of new people—non-Christian friends and extended family—available to them for an effective witness. These old friends and family are the ones most likely to notice the changes that becoming a Christian is bringing into a new believer's life, and be open in new ways to hear the gospel.

The following story illustrates what can happen. Beverly McCall and her witnessing team from Hillview Church, DePew, New York, visited Carol, a new resident in the community and the mother of a teenager who had attended Hillview Church. Because of marital problems, Carol was the only supporting adult in her family. As the team shared the gospel with her, Carol was impressed with the fact that God loved her and offered her eternal life. That evening she decided to trust Christ, and prayed to receive the gift of eternal life.

Carol grew rapidly in her new faith and began to bring her friends, relatives, and neighbors to church with her. She invited the witnessing team from church back to her home to share the gospel with her friends and relatives as she had them over for dessert.

The first to trust Christ were Carol's five children. Several of the older ones were baptized into the church. On another visit Carol's sister became a member of God's family. The following week, Carol invited two teams to her house. She had invited her parents. While one team met with her sister for follow-up discussion, the other team shared the gospel with her parents. Both chose to place their faith in Christ.

The chain of relationships continued. The gospel was shared the following weeks and months with Carol's brother-in-law, her sister-in-law's sister, neighbors of her parents, seven friends of her children, two neighbors next door, a cousin and her son, and other friends, all of whom prayed to receive the gift of new life in Christ.

While there were some who have not yet responded in faith, twenty-seven persons thus far have made commitments to Christ as a result of Carol's commitment. They are being incorporated into the congregation as they participate regularly. Carol and her sister-in-law are now also trainees in the evangelism training program of the church. [1]

If the opportunities for witness are greatest for the newest Christians, it is wiser to help them to share how and why Christ has helped them rather than to instruct them to abandon all their old friends and family in order to "be separate from the world" as we sometimes have.

Consider the results of evangelism training for planting new churches. If members could be trained in evangelism, the mobility of people in our time could become an aid to the growth of the church. Members who move away from their congregations would be less likely to lapse into indifference. The story of the church in Antioch (Acts 11:19-21) could be repeated in many places if we learned to share the Lord Jesus with the "Greeks" in our new homes as well as the "Jews" we might meet there. 1 Peter 3:15 clearly reminds us to be prepared at all times to give the reason for the hope that is in us.

Aspects of witness to be included in training. An effective witness needs to be appropriate to the situation and authentically communicated. That means knowing how to communicate in an understandable way. It means sharing about Christ as authentically as we might share about our favorite friend or our favorite hobby. With someone who knows little or nothing about our hobby we may begin explaining quite differently than when we share with a new acquaintance who has the same hobby.

The first thing we may need to learn in being a witness is how to listen. Are we really "present" to others when we are with them? Some of us may need to learn more social and conversational skills, but the quality of our relationships and the quality of our sharing is far more important. This is basic to the training we need.

One difficulty in learning may be related to negative associations we have with "witnessing" itself. In our minds we may still carry around a caricatured notion of witnessing that we have heard about or seen or experienced at some point in our lives. The fact that some Christians have been rude in their witnessing should not, however, keep us from learning to witness in a more Christlike manner. Learning to exercise simple courtesy in our witnessing is obviously important. We need to respect the feelings of others. We do not promote the cause of Christ by embarrassing people by our insensitivity even for the sake of the gospel.

Another difficulty in our learning may lie in the fact that faith in Christ is really a very personal matter and we hesitate to "invade" the privacy of another's life. We may feel that we have no right to "impose" our "opinions" on another. Actually, the gospel is not an opinion. Evangelism done with Christian sensitivity is not a matter of imposing opinions on others. The biggest favor we can do for anyone is to introduce them to Christ! Our training must help us to understand the difference between opinion and the gospel.

One of the real reasons we may draw back from encounters as personal as evangelism may involve, is our discomfort with closeness to another person. Even within our families where we might be expected to have closeness, some of us are distant and reserved. Closeness even there is uncomfortable for us. Our own fear of closeness can make evangelism difficult for us. We may need help to gain greater freedom in our own selves for close relationships.

Fear of rejection is the reason most commonly stated by Christians who have difficulty actually getting involved in evangelism. Once we do begin to learn and do get involved with others, however, we discover that we have usually greatly exaggerated the fear of rejection in our imagination.

Our training should help us to understand better how persons become believers. The person who has the privilege of helping a new believer make a personal commitment to Christ is usually only one of a number of persons who have had a part in influencing that person toward Christ. Very few new believers make a personal commitment to Christ as the result of their relationship with only one person. Often a meaningful and trusting relationship has developed with someone who is Christian, and the new believer experiences love and acceptance that draws him or her nearer to Christ. Such love and acceptance, however, have likely also been communicated by a number of other Christians in various ways, even though primarily one person may finally assist the new person in "opening the door" to Christ as Savior and Lord of his or her life.

How can we train for evangelism? A first step might be to

identify a person in the congregation who could work closely with the pastor as a director of outreach. One of the major responsibilities of this person would be to work with others in a training process.

This training process might begin with a study of evangelism. Such a study can give persons the opportunity to re-examine beliefs, correct some of their misconceptions, and sharpen their conceptual knowledge of evangelism. There are several helpful studies now available. (See discussion suggestions.)

While offering classes for training is helpful, it has been discovered by a few congregations that one to one "teacher and disciple" training plans are especially effective when they are carefully supervised by pastoral leaders. These plans are sometimes called "Paul-Timothy and Eunice-Lois" programs. They are especially helpful when they pair off new believers with more mature Christians.

If we stay in the classroom, however, most of us will probably not really learn to do evangelism. We need to learn by doing. We can read books about swimming, listen to lectures about swimming, and discuss swimming endlessly, but unless we actually get in the water we will not really learn to swim. Art McPhee, in *Friendship Evangelism,* likens learning to witness to learning to drive a car. At first someone explains to us how to drive. Then he may drive so we can observe him. On our first trip behind the wheel he may ride along beside us. We must concentrate on every move and watch very closely lest we drive into the ditch! But each time we drive the car we feel more at home with it. We are learning by doing.

These analogies remind us of the importance of several elements in the training process which have usually overlooked in the church. The first is the tremendous significance of models. We learn more about life from the example of others than we usually realize. But how many of us have had the opportunity to observe someone in the church doing what we wanted to learn to do—as an observer? How many of us, for example, have been with an experienced person as he practiced the art of sharing the gospel effectively person to person?

For training in evangelism we need good models from whom we can learn. Because evangelism is not simply a matter of skill—that is, learning what to say and how to say it—the importance of models becomes even more important. Learning to share our faith involves learning to relate to people and growing in our own Christian lives. There is no more helpful way to learn than to watch others whose example shows us in real life ways.

The second element so important in training for evangelism is the opportunity to continue to learn by doing—under supervision. Most of us find it difficult in the church to be subject to one another. This often becomes evident in the difficulty we have either to receive or to give the kind of honest, but helpful, supervision that can really change our ways. How do we tell a dear brother that the way he witnesses turns people against the gospel more than it helps them to turn toward Christ in trust and love? How do we help him to see some things in himself that cause others to take offense at his witness? A training program that involves the learner in step by step learning by doing, that includes loving confrontation as well as affirmation, and that has a modeling supervisor with a "learner's attitude" helps us to be more honest and helpful to one another.

Supervision helps us to "learn how to learn from our experience." The cliché "experience is the best teacher" is true only if we can learn to learn from our experience. Unless we do, we repeat the same mistakes in our experience over and over. We all need the help of others to reflect on our experiences. In a helpful training plan there is provision for reflecting very concretely on our experience, trusting the Holy Spirit to give us the insights we need.

The supervision to which we submit may be in a covenanted group as well as with an experienced person from whom we seek to learn. Such a group can become a caring group where needs are honestly shared and remembered in prayer. People learn to help one another and to love one another as they enter into the common experience of learning. Each time I asked the groups I helped to train what the training had meant for them, the strongest reply was that they felt they had grown more spiritually than in any other five-month period. They had grown more in their knowledge of the Bible than in any classroom experience. I had expected that they would have begun to learn to witness. But I was surprised at first to discover that the training process had been such a strong nurturing experience in other ways as well.

We learn slowly. Our ways of doing things change slowly. This is especially true if we have some old patterns to unlearn. The old "ruts" are often so deep that it takes months, even years, for us to change and to learn. For this reason a weekend workshop is hardly ever a sufficient training experience. It can be one helpful step in the training process, but training really needs to be ongoing in our local setting.

Jesus is our example of a master trainer.[2] For three years He modeled what a Spirit-led ministry is. The twelve He had chosen were given many opportunities to learn by doing. He took them aside to reflect with them about their experience. They learned much from Him because of the interaction of the group. When they were filled with the Holy Spirit on the Day of Pentecost, the Spirit reminded them of the things Jesus had taught them, enabled them to carry on the ministry they had begun to learn from Jesus, and now taught them more and more. The Holy Spirit is still our teacher and our trainer as we open ourselves to Him to learn and to change and to grow.

DISCUSSION

1. Read Luke 10:1-20. How did Jesus train His disciples for this particular mission?
2. What comments or questions do you wish to raise after reading this chapter?
3. Some helpful guides for further classroom group study in evangelism are:
   Augsburger, David, *Communicating Good News* (with teacher's guide), (Herald Press, 1972).

McPhee, Art, *Friendship Evangelism* (with leader's guide), (Zondervan, 1978).

Rinker, Rosalind, *You Can Witness with Confidence* (Zondervan, 1962).

Notes

[1] *Evangelism Explosion III Update* (November 1978), p. 11.

[2] See Robert E. Coleman, *The Master Plan of Evangelism* (Old Tappan, New Jersey: Fleming H. Revell, 1964), for an excellent description of Jesus' training of His disciples for their mission.